The Best 100 Poems of Les Murray

Les Murray

Copyright Page from the Original Book

Published by Black Inc.,
an imprint of Schwartz Media Pty Ltd
37–39 Langridge Street
Collingwood VIC 3066 Australia
email: enquiries@blackincbooks.com
http://www.blackincbooks.com

National Library of Australia Cataloguing-in-Publication entry

Murray, Les A. (Les Allan), 1938-
The best 100 poems of Les Murray / Les Murray.
ISBN: 9781863955843 (hbk.)
Australian poetry.
A821.3

Printed in China by 1010 Printing International.

To the glory of God

DRIVING THROUGH SAWMILL TOWNS

1

In the high cool country,
having come from the clouds,
down a tilting road
into a distant valley,
you drive without haste. Your windscreen parts the forest,
swaying and glancing, and jammed midday brilliance
crouches in clearings...
then you come across them,
the sawmill towns, bare hamlets built of boards
with perhaps a store,
perhaps a bridge beyond
and a little sidelong creek alive with pebbles.

2

The mills are roofed with iron, have no walls:
you look straight in as you pass, see lithe men working,

the swerve of a winch,
dim dazzling blades advancing
through a trolley-borne trunk
till it sags apart
in a manifold sprawl of weatherboards and battens.

The men watch you pass:
when you stop your car and ask them for directions,
tall youths look away–
it is the older men who
come out in blue singlets and talk softly to you.

Beside each mill, smoke trickles out of mounds of ash and sawdust.

3

You glide on through town,
your mudguards damp with cloud.
The houses there wear verandahs out of shyness,
all day in calendared kitchens, women listen
for cars on the road,
lost children in the bush,
a cry from the mill, a footstep–
nothing happens.

The half-heard radio sings
its song of sidewalks.

Sometimes a woman, sweeping her front step,
or a plain young wife at a tankstand fetching water
in a metal bucket will turn round and gaze
at the mountains in wonderment,
looking for a city.

4

Evenings are very quiet. All around
the forest is there.
As night comes down, the houses watch each
 other:
a light going out in a window here has meaning.

You speed away through the upland,
glare through towns
and are gone in the forest, glowing on far hills.

On summer nights
ground-crickets sing and pause.
In the dark of winter, tin roofs sough with rain,
downpipes chafe in the wind, agog with water.
Men sit after tea
by the stove while their wives talk, rolling a dead
 match
between their fingers,
thinking of the future.

AN ABSOLUTELY ORDINARY RAINBOW

The word goes round Repins,
the murmur goes round Lorenzinis,
at Tattersalls, men look up from sheets of
 numbers,

the Stock Exchange scribblers forget the chalk in their hands
and men with bread in their pockets leave the Greek Club:
There's a fellow crying in Martin Place. They can't stop him.

The traffic in George Street is banked up for half a mile
and drained of motion. The crowds are edgy with talk
and more crowds come hurrying. Many run in the back streets
which minutes ago were busy main streets, pointing:
There's a fellow weeping down there. No one can stop him.

The man we surround, the man no one approaches
simply weeps, and does not cover it, weeps
not like a child, not like the wind, like a man
and does not declaim it, nor beat his breast, nor even
sob very loudly – yet the dignity of his weeping

holds us back from his space, the hollow he makes about him
in the midday light, in his pentagram of sorrow,
and uniforms back in the crowd who tried to seize him
stare out at him, and feel, with amazement, their minds
longing for tears as children for a rainbow.

Some will say, in the years to come, a halo
or force stood around him. There is no such thing.
Some will say they were shocked and would have
 stopped him
but they will not have been there. The fiercest
 manhood,
the toughest reserve, the slickest wit amongst us

trembles with silence, and burns with unexpected
judgements of peace. Some in the concourse scream
who thought themselves happy. Only the smallest
 children
and such as look out of Paradise come near him
and sit at his feet, with dogs and dusty pigeons.

Ridiculous, says a man near me, and stops
his mouth with his hands, as if it uttered vomit–
and I see a woman, shining, stretch her hand
and shake as she receives the gift of weeping;
as many as follow her also receive it

and many weep for sheer acceptance, and more
refuse to weep for fear of all acceptance,
but the weeping man, like the earth, requires nothing,
the man who weeps ignores us, and cries out
of his writhen face and ordinary body

not words, but grief, not messages, but sorrow,
hard as the earth, sheer, present as the sea–
and when he stops, he simply walks between us

mopping his face with the dignity of one
man who has wept, and now has finished weeping.

Evading believers, he hurries off down Pitt Street.

KISS OF THE WHIP

In Cardiff, off Saint Mary's Street,
there in the porn shops you could get
a magazine called Kiss of the Whip.
I used to pretend I'd had poems in it.

Kiss of the Whip. I never saw it.
I might have encountered familiar skills
having been raised in a stockwhip culture.
Grandfather could dock a black snake's head,

Stanley would crack the snake for preference
leap from his horse grab whirl and jolt!
the popped head hummed from his one-shot slingshot.
The whips themselves were black, fine-braided,

arm-coiling beasts that could suddenly flourish
and cut a cannibal strip from a bull
(millisecond returns) or idly behead an
ant on the track. My father did that.

A knot in the lash would kill a rabbit.
There were decencies: good dogs and children
were flogged with the same lash doubled back.

A horsehair plait on the tip for a cracker

sharpened the note. For ten or twelve thousand
years this was the sonic barrier's
one human fracture. Whip-cracking is that:
thonged lightning making the leanest thunder.

When black snakes go to Hell they are
affixed by their fangs to carved whip-handles
and fed on nothing but noonday heat,
sweat and flowing rumps and language.

They writhe up dust-storms for revenge
and send them roaring where creature comfort's
got with a touch of the lash. And that
is a temple yard that will bear more cleansing

before, through droughts and barracks, those
lax, quiet-speaking, sudden fellows
emerge where skill unbraids from death
and mastering, in Saint Mary's Street.

THE BROAD BEAN SERMON

Beanstalks, in any breeze, are a slack church parade
without belief, saying *trespass against us* in unison,
recruits in mint Air Force dacron, with unbuttoned
 leaves.

Upright with water like men, square in stem-section

they grow to great lengths, drink rain, keel over all ways,
kink down and grow up afresh, with proffered new greenstuff.

Above the cat-and-mouse floor of a thin bean forest
snails hang rapt in their food, ants hurry through several dimensions:
spiders tense and sag like little black flags in their cordage.

Going out to pick beans with the sun high as fence-tops, you find
plenty, and fetch them. An hour or a cloud later
you find shirtfulls more. At every hour of daylight

appear more that you missed: ripe, knobbly ones, fleshy-sided,
thin-straight, thin-crescent, frown-shaped, bird-shouldered, boat-keeled ones,
beans knuckled and single-bulged, minute green dolphins at suck,

beans upright like lecturing, outstretched like blessing fingers
in the incident light, and more still, oblique to your notice
that the noon glare or cloud-light or afternoon slants will uncover

till you ask yourself Could I have overlooked so many, or
do they form in an hour? unfolding into reality
like templates for subtly broad grins, like unique caught expressions,

like edible meanings, each sealed around with a string
and affixed to its moment, an unceasing colloquial assembly,
the portly, the stiff, and those lolling in pointed green slippers...

Wondering who'll take the spare bagfulls, you grin with happiness
–it is your health – you vow to pick them all
even the last few, weeks off yet, misshapen as toes.

THE MITCHELLS

I am seeing this: two men are sitting on a pole
they have dug a hole for and will, after dinner, raise
I think for wires. Water boils in a prune tin.
Bees hum their shift in unthinning mists of white

bursaria blossom, under the noon of wattles.
The men eat big meat sandwiches out of a styrofoam
box with a handle. One is overheard saying:
drought that year. Yes. Like trying to farm the road.

The first man, if asked, would say *I'm one of the Mitchells.*
The other would gaze for a while, dried leaves in his palm,
and looking up, with pain and subtle amusement,

say *I'm one of the Mitchells.* Of the pair, one has been rich
but never stopped wearing his oil-stained felt hat. Nearly everything
they say is ritual. Sometimes the scene is an avenue.

EMPLOYMENT FOR THE CASTES IN ABEYANCE

I was a translator at the Institute:
fair pay, clean work, and a bowerbird's delight
of theory and fact to keep the forebrain supple.

I was Western Europe. *Beiträge, reviste,*
dissertaties, rapports turned English under my
one-fingered touch. Teacup-and-Remington days.

It was a job like Australia: peace and cover,
a recourse for exiles, poets, decent spies,
for plotters who meant to rise from the dead with their circle.

I was getting over a patch of free-form living:

flat food round the midriff, long food up your sleeves–
castes in abeyance, we exchanged these stories.

My Chekhovian colleague who worked as if under
 surveillance
would tell me tales of real life in Peking and Shanghai
and swear at the genders subsumed in an equation.

The trade was uneasy about computers, back then:
if they could be taught not to render, say, *out of sight*
out of mind as *invisible lunatic*

they might supersede us – not
because they'd be better. More on principle.
Not that our researchers were unkindly folk:

one man on exchange from Akademgorod
told me about Earth's crustal plates, their ponderous
inevitable motion, collisions that raised mountain
 chains,

the continents rode on these Marxian turtles, it
 seemed;
another had brought slow death to a billion rabbits,
a third team had bottled the essence of rain on dry
 ground.

They were translators, too, our scientists:
they were translating the universe into science,
believing that otherwise it had no meaning.

Leaving there, I kept my Larousse and my
 Leutseligkeit
and I heard that machine translation never
 happened:
language defeated it. We are a language species.

I gather this provoked a shift in science,
that having become a side, it then changed sides
and having collapsed, continued at full tempo.

Prince Obolensky succeeded me for a time
but he soon returned to Fiji to teach Hebrew.
In the midst of life, we are in employment:

seek, travel and print, seek-left-right-travel-and-
 bang
as the Chinese typewriter went which I saw
 working
when I was a translator in the Institute.

THE BULADELAH-TAREE HOLIDAY SONG CYCLE

1

The people are eating dinner in that country north
 of Legge's Lake;
behind flywire and venetians, in the dimmed cool,
 town people eat Lunch.

Plying knives and forks with a peek-in sound, with a tuck-in sound,
they are thinking about relatives and inventory, they are talking about customers and visitors.
In the country of memorial iron, on the creek-facing hills there,
they are thinking about bean plants, and rings of tank water, of growing a pumpkin by Christmas;
rolling a cigarette, they say thoughtfully Yes, and their companion nods, considering.
Fresh sheets have been spread and tucked tight, childhood rooms have been seen to,

for this is the season when children return with their children
to the place of Bingham's Ghost, of the Old Timber Wharf, of the Big Flood That Time,
the country of the rationalized farms, of the day-and-night farms, and of the Pitt Street farms,
of the Shire Engineer and many other rumours, of the tractor crankcase furred with chaff,
the places of sitting down near ferns, the snake-fear places, the cattle-crossing-long-ago places.

2

It is the season of the Long Narrow City; it has crossed the Myall, it has entered the North Coast,

that big stunning snake; it is looped through the
hills, burning all night there.
Hitching and flying on the downgrades,
processionally balancing on the climbs,
it echoes in O'Sullivan's Gap, in the tight coats of
the flooded-gum trees;
the tops of palms exclaim at it unmoved, there
near Wootton.
Glowing all night behind the hills, with a
north-shifting glare, burning behind the hills;
through Coolongolook, through Wang Wauk, across
the Wallamba,
the booming tarred pipe of the holiday slows and
spurts again; Nabiac chokes in glassy wind,
the forests on Kiwarrak dwindle in cheap light;
Tuncurry and Forster swell like cooking oil.
The waiting is buffed, in timber villages off the
highway, the waiting is buffeted:
the fumes of fun hanging above ferns; crime
flashes in strange windscreens, in the time of the
Holiday.
Parasites weave quickly through the long gut that
paddocks shine into;
powerful makes surging and pouncing: the police,
collecting Revenue.
The heavy gut winds over the Manning, filling
northward, digesting the towns, feeding the towns;
they all become the narrow city, they join it;
girls walking close to murder discard, with
excitement, their names.

Crossing Australia of the sports, the narrow city,
 bringing home the children.

3

It is good to come out after driving and walk on
 bare grass;
walking out, looking all around, relearning that
 country.
Looking out for snakes, and looking out for rabbits
 as well;
going into the shade of myrtles to try their cupped
 climate, swinging by one hand around them,
in that country of the Holiday...
stepping behind trees to the dam, as if you had a
 gun,
to that place of the Wood Duck,
to that place of the Wood Duck's Nest,
proving you can still do it; looking at the duck who
 hasn't seen you,
the mother duck who'd run Catch Me (broken wing)
 I'm Fatter (broken wing), having hissed to her
 children.

4

The birds saw us wandering along.
Rosellas swept up crying out *we think we think;*
 they settled farther along;

knapping seeds off the grass, under dead trees where
 their eggs were, walking around on their fingers,
flying on into the grass.
The heron lifted up his head and elbows; the magpie
 stepped aside a bit,
angling his chopsticks into pasture, turning things
 over in his head.
At the place of the Plough Handles, of the Apple Trees
 Bending Over, and of the Cattlecamp,
there the vealers are feeding; they are loosely at
 work, facing everywhere.
They are always out there, and the forest is always
 on the hills;
around the sun are turning the wedgetail eagle and
 her mate, that dour brushhook-faced family:
they settled on Deer's Hill away back when the sky
 was opened,
in the bull-oak trees way up there, the place of fur
 tufted in the grass, the place of bone-turds.

5

The Fathers and the Great-grandfathers, they are
 out in the paddocks all the time, they live out there,
at the place of the Rail Fence, of the Furrows Under
 Grass, at the place of the Slab Chimney.
We tell them that clearing is complete, an outdated
 attitude, all over;
we preach without a sacrifice, and are ignored;
 flowering bushes grow dull to our eyes.

We begin to go up on the ridge, talking together,
 looking at the kino-coloured ants,
at the yard-wide sore of their nest, that kibbled peak,
 and the workers heaving vast stalks up there,
the brisk compact workers; jointed soldiers pour out
 then, tense with acid; several probe the mouth of a
 lost gin bottle;

Innuendo, we exclaim, *literal minds!* and go on up
 the ridge, announced by finches;
passing the place of the Dingo Trap, and that farm
 hand it caught, and the place of the Cowbails,
we come to the road and watch heifers,
little unjoined Devons, their teats hidden in fur, and
 the cousin with his loose-slung stockwhip driving
 them.
We talk with him about rivers and the lakes; his
 polished horse is stepping nervously,
printing neat omegas in the gravel, flexing its skin to
 shake off flies;
his big sidestepping horse that has kept its stones;
 it recedes gradually, bearing him;
we murmur *stone-horse* and *devilry* to the grinners
 under grass.

6

Barbecue smoke is rising at Legge's Camp; it is
 steaming into the midday air,

all around the lake shore, at the Broadwater, it is going up among the paperbark trees,
a heat-shimmer of sauces, rising from tripods and flat steel, at that place of the cone shells,
at that place of the Seagrass, and the tiny segmented things swarming in it, and of the Pelican.
Dogs are running around disjointedly; water escapes from their mouths,
confused emotions from their eyes; humans snarl at them Gwanout and Hereboy, not varying their tone much;
the impoverished dog people, suddenly sitting down to nuzzle themselves; toddlers side with them:
toddlers, running away purposefully at random, among cars, into big drownie water (come back, Cheryl-Ann!).
They rise up as charioteers, leaning back on the tow-bar; all their attributes bulge at once:
swapping swash shoulder-wings for the white-sheeted shoes that bear them,
they are skidding over the flat glitter, stiff with grace, for once not travelling to arrive.
From the high dunes over there, the rough blue distance, at length they come back behind the boats,
and behind the boats' noise, cartwheeling, or sitting down, into the lake's warm chair;
they wade ashore and eat with the families, putting off that uprightness, that assertion,

eating with the families who love equipment, and
 the freedom from equipment,
with the fathers who love driving, and lighting a fire
 between stones.

7

Shapes of children were moving in the standing corn,
 in the child-labour districts;
coloured flashes of children, between the green and
 parching stalks, appearing and disappearing.
Some places, they are working, racking off each cob
 like a lever, tossing it on the heaps;
other places, they are children of child-age, there
 playing jungle:
in the tiger-striped shade, they are firing hoehandle
 machine-guns, taking cover behind fat pumpkins;
in other cases, it is Sunday and they are lovers.
They rise and walk together in the sibilance, finding
 single rows irksome, hating speech now,
or, full of speech, they swap files and follow defiles,
 disappearing and appearing;
near the rain-grey barns, and the children building
 cattleyards beside them;
the standing corn, gnawed by pouched and rodent
 mice; generations are moving among it,
the parrot-hacked, medicine-tasselled corn,
 ascending all the creek flats, the wire-fenced
 alluvials,

going up in patches through the hills, towards the
 Steep Country.

8

Forests and State Forests, all down off the steeper
 country; mosquitoes are always living in there:
they float about like dust motes and sink down, at
 the places of the Stinging Tree,
and of the Staghorn Fern; the males feed on
 plant-stem fluid, absorbing that watery ichor;
the females meter the air, feeling for the
 warm-blooded smell, needing blood for their eggs.
They find the dingo in his sleeping-place, they find
 his underbelly and his anus;
they find the possum's face, they drift up the
 ponderous pleats of the fig tree, way up into its
 rigging,
the high camp of the fruit bats; they feed on the
 membranes and ears of bats; tired wings cuff air at
 them;
their eggs burning inside them, they alight on the
 muzzles of cattle,
the half-wild bush cattle, there at the place of the
 Sleeper Dump, at the place of the Tallowwoods.
The males move about among growth tips; ingesting
 solutions, they crouch intently;
the females sing, needing blood to breed their young;
 their singing is in the scrub country;

their tune comes to the name-bearing humans, who dance to it and irritably grin at it.

9

The warriors are cutting timber with brash chainsaws;
they are trimming hardwood pit-props and loading them;
Is that an order? they hoot at the peremptory lorry driver, who laughs; he is also a warrior.
They are driving long-nosed tractors, slashing pasture in the dinnertime sun;
they are fitting tappets and valves, the warriors, or giving finish to a surfboard.
Addressed on the beach by a pale man, they watch waves break and are reserved, refusing pleasantry;
they joke only with fellow warriors, chaffing about try-ons and the police, not slighting women.
Making Timber a word of power, Con-rod a word of power, Sense a word of power, the Regs. a word of power,
they know belt-fed from spring-fed; they speak of being *stiff,* and being *history;*
the warriors who have killed, and the warriors who eschewed killing,
the solemn, the drily spoken, the life peerage of endurance; drinking water from a tap,
they watch boys who think hard work a test, and boys who think it is not a test.

10

Now the ibis are flying in, hovering down on the wetlands,
on those swampy paddocks around Darawank, curving down in ragged dozens,
on the riverside flats along the Wang Wauk, on the Boolambayte pasture flats,
and away towards the sea, on the sand moors, at the place of the Jabiru Crane;
leaning out of their wings, they step down; they take out their implement at once,
out of its straw wrapping, and start work; they dab grasshopper and ground-cricket
with nonexistence ... spiking the ground and puncturing it ... they swallow down the outcry of a frog;
they discover titbits kept for them under cowmanure lids, small slow things.
Pronging the earth, they make little socket noises, their thoughtfulness jolting down and up suddenly;
there at Bunyah, along Firefly Creek, and up through Germany,
the ibis are all at work again, thin-necked ageing men towards evening; they are solemnly all back
at Minimbah, and on the Manning, in the rye-and-clover irrigation fields;
city storemen and accounts clerks point them out to their wives,

remembering things about themselves, and about the
ibis.

11

Abandoned fruit trees, moss-tufted, spotted with dim
lichen paints; the fruit trees of the Grandmothers,
they stand along the creekbanks, in the old home
paddocks, where the houses were,
they are reached through bramble-grown front gates,
they creak at dawn behind burnt skillions,
at Belbora, at Bucca Wauka, away in at Burrell Creek,
at Telararee of the gold-sluices.
The trees are split and rotten-elbowed; they bear the
old-fashioned summer fruits,
the annual bygones: china pear, quince, persimmon;
the fruit has the taste of former lives, of sawdust and
parlour song, the tang of Manners;
children bite it, recklessly,
at what will become for them the place of the Slab
Wall, and of the Coal Oil Lamp,
the place of moss-grit and swallows' nests, the place
of the Crockery.

12

Now the sun is an applegreen blindness through the
swells, a white blast on the sea face, flaking and
shoaling;

now it is burning off the mist; it is emptying the density of trees, it is spreading upriver,
hovering about the casuarina needles, there at Old Bar and Manning Point;
flooding the island farms, it abolishes the milkers' munching breath
as they walk towards the cowyards; it stings a bucket here, a teatcup there.
Morning steps into the world by ever more southerly gates; shadows weaken their north skew
on Middle Brother, on Cape Hawke, on the dune scrub toward Seal Rocks;
steadily the heat is coming on, the butter-water time, the clothes-sticking time;
grass covers itself with straw; abandoned things are thronged with spirits;
everywhere wood is still with strain; birds hiding down the creek galleries, and in the cockspur canes;
the cicada is hanging up her sheets; she takes wing off her music-sheets.
Cars pass with a rational zoom, panning quickly towards Wingham,
through the thronged and glittering, the shale-topped ridges, and the cattlecamps,
towards Wingham for the cricket, the ball knocked hard in front of smoked-glass ranges, and for the drinking.

In the time of heat, the time of flies around the mouth, the time of the west verandah;
looking at that umbrage along the ranges, on the New England side;
clouds begin assembling vaguely, a hot soiled heaviness on the sky, away there towards Gloucester;
a swelling up of clouds, growing there above Mount George, and above Tipperary;
far away and hot with light; sometimes a storm takes root there, and fills the heavens rapidly;
darkening, boiling up and swaying on its stalks, pulling this way and that, blowing round by Krambach;
coming white on Bulby, it drenches down on the paddocks, and on the wire fences;
the paddocks are full of ghosts, and people in cornbag hoods approaching;
lights are lit in the house; the storm veers mightily on its stem, above the roof; the hills uphold it;
the stony hills guide its dissolution; gullies opening and crumbling down, wrenching tussocks and rolling them;
the storm carries a greenish-grey bag; perhaps it will find hail and send it down, starring cars, flattening tomatoes,
in the time of the Washaways, of the dead trunks braiding water, and of the Hailstone Yarns.

13

The stars of the holiday step out all over the sky.
People look up at them, out of their caravan doors
 and their campsites;
people look up from the farms, before going back;
 they gaze at their year's worth of stars.
The Cross hangs head-downward, out there over
 Markwell;
it turns upon the Still Place, the pivot of the Seasons,
 with one shoulder rising:
'Now I'm beginning to rise, with my Pointers and my
 Load...'
hanging eastwards, it shines on the sawmills and the
 lakes, on the glasses of the Old People.
Looking at the Cross, the galaxy is over our left
 shoulder, slung up highest in the east;
there the Dog is following the Hunter; the Dog Star
 pulsing there above Forster; it shines down on the
 Bikies,
and on the boat-hire sheds, there at the place of the
 Oyster; the place of the Shark's Eggs and her Hide;
the Pleiades are pinned up high on the darkness, away
 back above the Manning;
they are shining on the Two Blackbutt Trees, on the
 rotted river wharves, and on the towns;
standing there, above the water and the lucerne flats,
 at the place of the Families;
their light sprinkles down on Taree of the Lebanese
 shops, it mingles with the streetlights and their glare.

People recover the starlight, hitching north,
travelling north beyond the seasons, into that country of the Communes, and of the Banana:
the Flying Horse, the Rescued Girl, and the Bull, burning steadily above that country.
Now the New Moon is low down in the west, that remote direction of the Cattlemen,
and of the Saleyards, the place of steep clouds, and of the Rodeo;
the New Moon who has poured out her rain, the moon of the Planting-times.
People go outside and look at the stars, and at the melonrind moon,
the Scorpion going down into the mountains, over there towards Waukivory, sinking into the tree-line,
in the time of the Rockmelons, and of the Holiday...
the Cross is rising on his elbow, above the glow of the horizon;
carrying a small star in his pocket, he reclines there brilliantly,
above the Alum Mountain, and the lakes threaded on the Myall River, and above the Holiday.

THE FUTURE

There is nothing about it. Much science fiction is set there
but is not about it. Prophecy is not about it.
It sways no yarrow stalks. And crystal is a mirror.
Even the man we nailed on a tree for a lookout

said little about it; he told us evil would come.
We see, by convention, a small living distance into it
but even that's a projection. And all our projections
fail to curve where it curves.

It is the black hole
out of which no radiation escapes to us.
The commonplace and magnificent roads of our lives
go on some way through cityscape and landscape
or steeply sloping, or scree, into that sheer fall
where everything will be that we have ever sent
 there,
compacted, spinning – except perhaps us, to see it.
It is said we see the start.

But, from here, there's a blindness.
The side-heaped chasm that will swallow all our
 present
blinds us to the normal sun that may be imagined
shining calmly away on the far side of it, for others
in their ordinary day. A day to which all our portraits,
ideals, revolutions, denim and deshabille
are quaintly heartrending. To see those people is
 impossible,
to greet them, mawkish. Nonetheless, I begin:
'When I was alive–'

and I am turned around
to find myself looking at a cheerful picnic party,
the women decently legless, in muslin and gloves,

the men in beards and weskits, with the long
cheroots and duck trousers of the better sort,
relaxing on a stone verandah. Ceylon, or Sydney.
And as I look, I know they are utterly gone,
each one on his day, with pillow, small bottles, mist,
with all the futures they dreamed or dealt in, going
down to that engulfment everything approaches;
with the man on the tree, they have vanished into
the Future.

THE FISHERMEN AT SOUTH HEAD

They have walked out as far as they can go on the
prow of the continent,
on the undercut white sandstone, the bowsprits of
the towering headland.
They project their long light canes
or raise them up to check and string, like quiet
archers.
Between casts they hold them couched,
a finger on the line, two fingers on a cigarette, the
reel cocked.

They watch the junction of smooth blue with far
matt-shining blue,
the join where clouds enter,
or they watch the wind-shape of their nylon
bend like a sail's outline
south towards, a mile away, the city's floating gruel
of gull-blown effluent.

Sometimes they glance north, at the people on that calf-coloured edge
lower than theirs, where the suicides come by taxi
and stretchers are winched up
later, under raining lights
but mostly their eyes stay level with the land-and-ocean glitter.

Where they stand, atop the centuries
of strata, they don't look down much
but feel through their tackle the talus-eddying
and tidal detail of that huge simple pulse
in the rock and their bones.

Through their horizontal poles they divine the creatures of ocean:
a touch, a dip, and a busy winding death gets started;
hands will turn for minutes, rapidly,
before, still opening its pitiful doors, the victim
dawns above the rim, and is hoisted in a flash above the suburbs

–or before the rod flips, to stand
trailing sworn-at gossamer.

On that highest dreadnought scarp, where the terra cotta
waves of bungalows stop, suspended at sky,
the hunters stand apart.

They encourage one another, at a distance, not by talk

but by being there, by unhooking now and then
a twist of silver for the creel, by a vaguely mutual
zodiac of cars TV windcheaters.
Braced, casual normality. Anything unshared,
a harlequin mask, a painted wand flourished at the sun,
would anger them. It is serious to be with humans.

QUINTETS FOR ROBERT MORLEY

Is it possible that hyperventilating
up Parnassus
I have neglected to pay tribute
to the Stone Age aristocracy? I refer to the fat.

We were probably the earliest
civilized, and civilizing, humans,
the first to win the leisure,
sweet boredom, life-enhancing sprawl that require style.

Tribesfolk spared us and cared for us
for good reasons. Our reasons.
As age's counterfeits, forerunners of the city,
we survived, and multiplied. Out of self-defence we invented the Self.

It’s likely we also invented some of love,
much of fertility (see the Willensdorf Venus)
parts of theology (divine feasting, Unmoved Movers)
likewise complexity, stateliness, the ox-cart and
 self-deprecation.

Not that the lists of pugnacity are bare
of stout fellows. Ask a Sumo.
Warriors taunt us still, and fear us:
in heroic war, we are apt to be the specialists and
 the generals.

But we do better in peacetime. For ourselves
we would spare the earth. We were the first
 moderns
after all, being like the Common Man
disqualified from tragedy. Accessible to shame,
 though, subtler than the tall,

we make reasonable rulers.
Never trust a lean meritocracy
nor the leader who has been lean;
only the lifelong big have the knack of wedding
 greatness with balance.

Never wholly trust the fat man
who lurks in the lean achiever
and in the defeated, yearning to get out.
He has not been through our initiations, he lacks
 the light feet.

Our having life abundantly
is equivocal, Robert, in hot climates
where the hungry watch us. I lack the light step
 then too.
How many of us, I wonder, walk those streets in
 terrible disguise?

So much climbing, on a spherical world;
had Newton not been a mere beginner at gravity
he might have asked how the apple got up there
in the first place. And so might have discerned an
 ampler physics.

TWO POEMS IN MEMORY OF MY MOTHER, MIRIAM MURRAY NÉE ARNALL

Born 23.5.1915, Died 19.4.1951

Weights

Not owning a cart, my father
in the drought years was a bowing
green hut of cattle feed, moving,
or gasping under cream cans. No weight
would he let my mother carry.

Instead, she wielded handles
in the kitchen and dairy, singing often,

gave saucepan-boiled injections
with her ward-sister skill, nursed neighbours,
scorned gossips, ran committees.

She gave me her factual tone,
her facial bones, her will,
not her beautiful voice
but her straightness and her clarity.

I did not know back then
nor for many years what it was,
after me, she could not carry.

Midsummer Ice

Remember how I used
to carry ice in from the road
for the ice chest, half running,
the white rectangle clamped in bare hands
the only utter cold
in all those summer paddocks?

How, swaying, I'd hurry it inside
en bloc and watering, with the butter
and the wrapped bread precarious on top of it?
'Poor Leslie,' you would say,
'your hands are cold as charity–'
You made me take the barrow
but uphill it was heavy.

We'd no tongs, and a bag
would have soaked and bumped, off balance.
I loved to eat the ice,
chip it out with the butcher knife's grey steel.
It stopped good things rotting
and it had a strange comb at its heart,
a splintered horizon rife with zero pearls.

But you don't remember.
A doorstep of numbed creek water the colour of tears
but you don't remember.
I will have to die before you remember.

MACHINE PORTRAITS WITH PENDANT SPACEMAN

for Valerie

The bulldozer stands short as a boot on its heel-high
 ripple soles;
it has toecapped stumps aside all day, scuffed earth
 and trampled rocks
making a hobnailed dyke downstream of raw clay
 shoals.
Its work will hold water. The man who bounced high
 on the box
seat, exercising levers, would swear a full frontal
 orthodox
oath to that. First he shaved off the grizzled scrub

with that front-end safety razor supplied by the school
 of hard knocks
then he knuckled down and ground his irons properly;
 they copped many a harsh rub.
At knock-off time, spilling thunder, he surfaced like
 a sub.

***

Speaking of razors, the workshop amazes with its
 strop,
its elapsing leather drive-belt angled to the slapstick
 flow
of fast work in the Chaplin age; tightened, it runs like
 syrup,
streams like a mill-sluice, fiddles like a glazed
 virtuoso.
With the straitlaced summary cut of Sam Brownes
 long ago
it is the last of the drawn lash and bullocking muscle
left in engineering. It's where the panther leaping,
 his swift shadow
and all such free images turned plastic. Here they
 dwindle, dense with oil,
like a skein between tough factory hands, pulley and
 diesel.

***

Shaking in slow low flight, with its span of many jets,

the combine seeder at nightfall swimming over flat
 land
is a style of machinery we'd imagined for the fictional
 planets:
in the high glassed cabin, above vapour-pencilling
 floodlights, a hand,
gloved against the cold, hunts along the medium-wave
 band
for company of Earth voices; it crosses speech garble
 music–
the Brandenburg Conch the Who the Illyrian High
 Command–
as seed wheat in the hoppers shakes down, being
 laced into the thick
night-dampening plains soil, and the stars waver out
 and stick.

***

Flags and a taut fence discipline the mountain pasture
where giant upturned mushrooms gape mildly at the
 sky
catching otherworld pollen. Poppy-smooth or
 waffle-ironed, each armature
distils wild and white sound. These, Earth's first
 antennae
tranquilly angled outwards, to a black, not a gold
 infinity,
swallow the millionfold numbers that print out as a
 risen

glorious Apollo. They speak control to satellites in high
bursts of algorithm. And some of them are tuned to win
answers to fair questions, viz. What is the Universe in?

***

How many metal-bra and trumpet-flaring film extravaganzas
underlie the progress of the space shuttle's Ground Transporter Vehicle
across macadam-surfaced Florida? Atop oncreeping house-high panzers,
towering drydock and ocean-liner decks, there perches a gridiron football
field in gradual motion; it is the god-platform; it sustains the bridal
skyscraper of liquid Cool, and the rockets borrowed from the Superman
and the bricked aeroplane of Bustout-and-return, all vertical,
conjoined and myth-huge, approaching the starred gantry where human
lightning will crack, extend, and vanish upwards from this caravan.

***

Gold-masked, the foetal warrior
unslipping on a flawless floor,
I backpack air; my life machine
breathes me head-Earthwards, speaks the Choctaw
of tech-talk that earths our discipline–

but the home world now seems outside-in;
I marvel that here background's so fore
and sheathe my arms in the unseen

a dream in images unrecalled
from any past takes me I soar
at the heart of fall on a drifting line

this is the nearest I have been
to oneness with the everted world
the unsinking leap the stone unfurled

***

In a derelict village picture show I will find a projector,
dust-matted, but with film in its drum magazines, and the lens
mysteriously clean. The film will be called *Insensate Violence,*
no plot, no characters, just shoot burn scream beg claw
bayonet trample brains – I will hit the reverse switch then, in conscience,

and the thing will run backwards, unlike its coeval the machine-gun;
blood will unspill, fighters lift and surge apart; horror will be undone
and I will come out to a large town, bright parrots round the saleyard pens
and my people's faces healed of a bitter sophistication.

***

The more I act, the stiller I become;
the less I'm lit, the more spellbound my crowd;
I accept all colours, and with a warming hum
I turn them white and hide them in a cloud.
To give long life is a power I'm allowed
by my servant, Death. I am what you can't sell
at the world's end – and if you're still beetle-browed
try some of my treasures: an adult bird in its shell
or a pink porker in his own gut, Fritz the Abstract Animal.

***

No riddles about a crane. This one drops a black clanger on cars
and the palm of its four-thumbed steel hand is a raptor of wrecked tubing;
the ones up the highway hoist porridgy concrete, long spars
and the local skyline; whether raising aloft on a string

bizarre workaday angels, or letting down a rotating
man on a sphere, these machines are inclined to
 maintain
a peace like world war, in which we turn over
 everything
to provide unceasing victories. Now the fluent lines
 stop, and strain
engrosses this tower on the frontier of junk, this
 crane.

***

Before a landscape sprouts those giant stepladders
 that pump oil
or before far out iron mosquitoes attach to the sea
there is this sortilege with phones that plug into
 mapped soil,
the odd gelignite bump to shake trucks, paper
 scribbling out serially
as men dial Barrier Reefs long enfolded beneath the
 geology
or listen for black Freudian beaches; they seek a
 miles-wide pustular
rock dome of pure Crude, a St Paul's-in-profundis.
 There are many
wrong numbers on the geophone, but it's brought us
 some distance, and by car.
Every machine has been love and a true answer.

***

Not a high studded ship boiling cauliflower under her keel
nor a ghost in bootlaced canvas – just a length of country road
afloat between two shores, winding wet wire rope reel-to-reel,
dismissing romance sternwards. Six cars and a hay truck are her load
plus a thoughtful human cast which could, in some dramatic episode,
become a world. All machines in the end join God's creation
growing bygone, given, changeless – but a river ferry has its timeless mode
from the grinding reedy outset; it enforces contemplation.
We arrive. We traverse depth in thudding silence. We go on.

SHOWER

From the metal poppy
this good blast of trance
arriving as shock, private cloudburst blazing down,
worst in a boarding-house greased tub, or a barrack with competitions,
best in a stall, this enveloping passion of Australians:
tropics that sweat for you, torrent that braces with its heat,
inflames you with its chill, action sauna, inverse bidet,

sleek vertical coruscating ghost of your inner river,
reminding all your fluids, streaming off your points, awakening
the tacky soap to blossom and ripe autumn, releasing the squeezed gardens,
smoky valet smoothing your impalpable overnight pyjamas off,
pillar you can step through, force-field absolving love's efforts,
nicest yard of the jogging track, speeding aeroplane minutely
steered with two controls, or trimmed with a knurled wheel.
Some people like to still this energy and lie in it,
stirring circles with their pleasure in it – but my delight's that toga
worn on either or both shoulders, fluted drapery, silk whispering to the tiles
with its spiralling frothy hem continuous round the gurgle-hole;
this ecstatic partner, dreamy to dance in slow embrace with
after factory-floor rock, or even to meet as Lot's abstracted
merciful wife on a rusty ship in dog latitudes,
sweetest dressing of the day in the dusty bush, this persistent
time-capsule of unwinding, this nimble straight well-wisher.
Only in England is its name an unkind word;

only in Europe is it enjoyed by telephone.

TIME TRAVEL

for Daniel

To revisit the spitfire world
of the duel, you put on a suit
of white body armour, a helmet
like an insect's composite eye
and step out like a space walker
under haloed lights, trailing a cord.

Descending, with nodding foil in hand
towards the pomander-and-cravat sphere
you meet the Opponent, for this journey
can only be accomplished by a pair
who semaphore and swap quick respect
before they set about their joint effect

which is making zeroes and serifs so
swiftly and with such sprung variety
that the long steels skid, clatter, zing,
switch, batter, bite, kiss and ring
in the complex rhythms of that society
with its warrior snare of comme il faut

that has you facing a starched beau
near stable walls on a misty morning,
striking, seeking the surrender in him,

the pedigree-flaw through which to pin him,
he probing for your own braggadocio,
confusion, ennui or inner fawning–

Seconds, holding stakes and cloths, look grim
and surge a step. Exchanges halt
for one of you stands, ageing horribly,
collapses, drowning from an entry
of narrow hurt. The other gulps hot chocolate
a trifle fast, but talking nonchalant–

a buzzer sounds. Heads are tucked
under arms, and you and he swap
curt nods in a more Christian century.

LOUVRES

In the banana zone, in the poinciana tropics
reality is stacked on handsbreadth shelving,
open and shut, it is ruled across with lines
as in a gleaming gritty exercise book.

The world is seen through a cranked or levered
weatherboarding of explosive glass
angled floor-to-ceiling. Horizons which metre
the dazzling outdoors into green-edged couplets.

In the louvred latitudes
children fly to sleep in triplanes, and
cool nights are eerie with retracting flaps.

Their houses stand aloft among bougainvillea,
covered bridges that lead down a shining hall
from love to mystery to breakfast,
from babyhood to moving-out day

and visitors shimmer up in columnar gauges
to touch lives lived behind gauze
in a lantern of inventory,
slick vector geometries glossing the months of rain.

There, nudity is dizzily cubist, and directions
have to include: stage left, add an inch of breeze
or: enter a glistening tendril.

Every building of jinked and slatted ledges
is at times a squadron of inside-out
helicopters, humming with rotor fans.

For drinkers under cyclonic pressure, such
a house can be a bridge of scythes–
groundlings scuffing by stop only for dénouements.

But everyone comes out on platforms of command
to survey cloudy flame-trees, the plain of streets, the future:
only then descending to the level of affairs

and if these things are done in the green season
what to do in the crystalline dry? Well
below in the struts of laundry is the four-wheel drive

vehicle in which to make an expedition
to the bush, or as we now say the Land,
the three quarters of our continent
set aside for mystic poetry.

FLOOD PLAINS ON THE COAST FACING ASIA

Hitching blur to a caged propeller
with its motor racket swelling
barroom to barrage, our aluminium
airboat has crossed the black coffee
lagoon and swum out onto
one enormous crinkling green.
Now like a rocket loudening
to liftoff, it erects the earsplitting
wigwam we must travel in
everywhere here, and starts skimming
at speed on the never-never
meadows of the monsoon wetland.

Birds lift, scattering before us
over the primeval irrigation,
leaf-running jacanas, twin-boomed
with supplicant bare feet for tails;
knob-headed magpie geese
row into the air ahead of us;
waterlilies lean away, to go
under as we overrun them

and resurrect behind us.
We leave at most a darker green
trace on the universal glittering
and, waterproof in cream and blue,
waterlilies on their stems, circling.

Our shattering car
crossing exposed and seeping spaces
brings us to finely stinking places,
yet whatever riceless paddies
we reach, of whatever grass,
there is always sheeting spray
underhull for our passage;
and the Intermediate Egret leaps
aloft out of stagnant colours
and many a double-barrelled crossbow
shoots vegetable breath emphatically
from the haunts of flaking buffalo;
water glinting everywhere, like ice,
we traverse speeds humans once reached
in such surroundings mainly
as soldiers, in the tropic wars.

At times, we fold our windtunnel
away, in its blackened steel sail
and sit, for talk and contemplation.
For instance, off the deadly islet,
a swamp-surrounded sandstone knoll
split, cabled, commissured
with fig trees' python roots.

Watched by distant plateau cliffs
stitched millennially in every crevice
with the bark-entubed dead
we do not go ashore.
Those hills are ancient stone gods
just beginning to be literature.

We release again the warring sound
of our peaceful tour, and go sledding
headlong through mounded paperbark
copses, on reaches of maroon
grit, our wake unravelling
over green curd where logs lie digesting
and over the breast-lifting deeps
of the file snake, whom the women here
tread on, scoop up, clamp head-first in their teeth
and jerk to death, then carry home as meat.

Loudest without speech, we shear
for miles on the paddock of nymphaeas
still hoisting up the paired pied geese,
their black goslings toddling below them.
We, a family with baby and two friends,
one swift metal skin above the food-chains,
the extensible wet life-chains of which
our civility and wake are one stretch,
the pelicans circling over us another
and the cat-napping peace of the secure,
of eagles, lions and two-year-old George
asleep beneath his pink linen hat as

we enter domains of flowering lotus.

In our propeller's stiffened silence
we stand up among scalloped leaves
that are flickering for hundreds of acres
on their deeper water. The lotus
prove a breezy nonhuman gathering
of this planet, with their olive-studded
rubbery cocktail glasses, loose carmine roses,
salmon buds like the five-fingertips-joined
gesture of summation, of *ecco!*
waist-high around us in all their greenery
on yeasty frog water. We receive this
sidelong, speaking our wiry language
in which so many others ghost and flicker.

We discuss Leichhardt's party and their qualities
when, hauling the year 1845
through here, with spearheads embedded in it,
their bullock drays reached and began skirting
this bar of literal water
after the desert months which had been
themselves a kind of swimming,
a salt undersea plodding, monster-haunted
with odd very pure surfacings.
We also receive, in drifts of calm
hushing, which fret the baby boy,
how the fuzzed gold innumerable cables
by which this garden hangs skyward
branch beneath the surface, like dreams.

The powerful dream of being harmless,
the many chains snapped and stretched hard for
 that:
both shimmer behind our run back
toward the escarpments where stallion-eyed
Lightning lives, who'd shiver all heights
down and make of the earth
one oozing, feeding peneplain.
Unprotected Lightning: there are his wild horses
and brolgas, and far heron not rising.
Suddenly we run over a crocodile.
On an unlilied deep, bare even
of minute water fern, it leaped out,
surged man-swift straight under us. We ran over it.
We circle back. Unhurt, it floats, peering
from each small eye turret, then annuls
buoyancy and merges subtly under,
swollen leathers becoming gargoyle stone,
chains of contour, with pineapple abdomen.

ROMAN CAGE-CUPS

Polish, at a constant curving interval, within
a layer of air between the inner and outer
skins of a glass beaker, leaving only odd struts
 integral.

Pause, and at the same ablative atomby-atom
rate, sculpt the outer shell to an openwork
of rings, or foliage, or a muscular Elysium–

It made for calm paste and a steady file
that one false stroke, one twitch could cost a year's time,
a good billet, your concubine. Only the cups were held noble.

Plebs and immigrants fashioned them, punters
who ate tavern-fried pike and talked Vulgate.
The very first might have been made as a stunt, as

the life-gambit of a slave. Or a joke on the feasting scene:
a wine-bowl no one coarsely drunk could handle
nor, since baseless, easily put down,

a marvel of undercutting, a glass vessel
so costly it would exact that Roman gravity,
draw blood, and feud, if grasped without suavity.

The one depicting Thracian Lycurgus
strangled by amorous vines for slighting Bacchus
could hardly have survived an old-time bacchanal.

The glass flowers of Harvard, monks' micro pen-lace, a chromosome
needled to grow wings on a horse (which they'd also have done),
the freely moving ivory dragons-inside-a-dragon

ball of Cathay – the impossible is a groove:

why else do we do it? Even some given a choice
would rather work the metaphors than live them, in
society.

But nothing, since sparkle became permanent in the
thumbs
and rib-cages of these craftsmen, has matched their
handiwork
for gentleness, or edge. They put the gape into
agapé,

these factory products, of all Rome's underground
Gothic:
cups transfigured by hand, too delicate to break.
Some, exported beyond the Rhine as a *mission*
civilisatrice, have survived complete and unchipped
a sesquimillennium longer than the trumpets (allude,
allude) of the arena. Rome's very hardest rock.

NOCTURNE

Brisbane, night-gathered, far away
estuarine imaginary city
of houses towering down one side
of slatted lights seen under leaves

confluence of ranginess with lush,
Brisbane, of rotogravure memory
approached by web lines of coke and grit
by sleepers racked in corridor trains

weatherboard incantatory city
of the timber duchess, the strapped port
in Auchenflower and Fortitude Valley
and bottletops spat in Vulture Street

greatest of the floodtime towns
that choked the dictionary with silt
and hung a navy in the tropic gardens.
Brisbane, on the steep green slope to war

brothel-humid headquarters city
where commandos and their allies fought
down café stairs, belt buckle and boot
and once with a rattletrap green gun.

In midnight nets, in mango bombings
Brisbane, storied and cable-fixed,
above your rum river, farewell and adieu
in marble on the hill of Toowong

by golfing pockets, by deep squared pockets
night heals the bubbled tar of day
and the crab moon, rising, reddens above
Brisbane, rotating far away.

THE DREAM OF WEARING SHORTS FOREVER

To go home and wear shorts forever

in the enormous paddocks, in that warm climate,
adding a sweater when winter soaks the grass,

to camp out along the river bends
for good, wearing shorts, with a pocketknife,
a fishing line and matches,

or there where the hills are all down, below the
 plain,
to sit around in shorts at evening
on the plank verandah–

If the cardinal points of costume
are Robes, Tat, Rig and Scunge,
where are shorts in this compass?

They are never Robes
as other bareleg outfits have been:
the toga, the kilt, the lava-lava
the Mahatma's cotton dhoti;

archbishops and field marshals
at their ceremonies never wear shorts.
The very word
means underpants in North America.

Shorts can be Tat,
Land-Rovering bush-environmental tat,
socio-political ripped-and-metal-stapled tat,
solidarity-with-the-Third-World tat tvam asi,

likewise track-and-field shorts worn to parties
and the further humid, modelling negligée
of the Kingdom of Flaunt,
that unchallenged aristocracy.

More plainly climatic, shorts
are farmers' rig leathery with salt and bonemeal,
are sailors' and branch bankers' rig,
the crisp golfing style
of our youngest male National Costume.

Mostly loosely, they are Scunge,
ancient Bengal bloomers or moth-eaten hot pants
worn with a former shirt,
feet, beach sand, hair
and a paucity of signals.

Scunge, which is real negligée
housework in a swimsuit, pyjamas worn all day,
is holiday, is freedom from ambition.
Scunge makes you invisible
to the world and yourself.

The entropy of costume,
scunge can get you conquered by more vigorous
 cultures
and help you to notice it less.

Satisfied ambition, defeat, true unconcern,
the wish and the knack for self-forgetfulness

all fall within the scunge ambit
wearing board shorts or similar;
it is a kind of weightlessness.

Unlike public nakedness, which in Westerners
is deeply circumstantial, relaxed as exam time,
artless and equal as the corsetry of a hussar regiment,

shorts and their plain like
are an angelic nudity,
spirituality with pockets!
A double updraft as you drop from branch to pool!

Ideal for getting served last
in shops of the temperate zone
they are also ideal for going home, into space,
into time, to farm the mind's Sabine acres
for product or subsistence.

Now that everyone who yearned to wear long pants
has essentially achieved them,
long pants, which have themselves been underwear
repeatedly, and underground more than once,
it is time perhaps to cherish the culture of shorts,

to moderate grim vigour
with the knobble of bare knees,
to cool bareknuckle feet in inland water,
slapping flies with a book on solar wind
or a patient bare hand, beneath the cadjiput trees,

to be walking meditatively
among green timber, through the grassy forest
towards a calm sea
and looking across to more of that great island
and the further topics.

POETRY AND RELIGION

Religions are poems. They concert
our daylight and dreaming mind, our
emotions, instinct, breath and native gesture

into the only whole thinking: poetry.
Nothing's said till it's dreamed out in words
and nothing's true that figures in words only.

A poem, compared with an arrayed religion,
may be like a soldier's one short marriage night
to die and live by. But that is a small religion.

Full religion is the large poem in loving repetition;
like any poem, it must be inexhaustible and complete
with turns where we ask Now why did the poet do
 that?

You can't pray a lie, said Huckleberry Finn;
you can't poe one either. It is the same mirror:
mobile, glancing, we call it poetry,

fixed centrally, we call it a religion,

and God is the poetry caught in any religion,
caught, not imprisoned. Caught as in a mirror

that he attracted, being in the world as poetry
is in the poem, a law against its closure.
There'll always be religion around while there is poetry

or a lack of it. Both are given, and intermittent,
as the action of those birds – crested pigeon, rosella parrot–
who fly with wings shut, then beating, and again shut.

JULY: MIDWINTER HAIRCUT

Now the world has stopped. Dead middle of the year.
Cloud all the colours of a worn-out dairy bucket
freeze-frames the whole sky. The only sun is down
intensely deep in the dam's bewhiskered mirror
and the white-faced heron hides in the drain with her spear.

Now the world has stopped, doors could be left open.
Only one fly came awake to the kitchen heater
this breakfast time, and supped on a rice bubble sluggishly.
No more will come inside out of the frost-crimped grass now.
Crime, too, sits in faraway cars. Phone lines drop at the horizon.

Now the world has stopped, what do we feel like doing?
The district's former haircutter, from the time before barbers, has shaved
and wants a haircut. So do I. No longer the munching hand clippers
with locks in their gears, nor the scissors more pointed than a beak
but the buzzing electric clipper, straight from its cardboard giftbox.

We'll sit under that on the broad-bottomed stool that was
the seat for fifty years of the district's only sit-down job,
the postmistress-telephonist's seat, where our poor greataunt
who trundled and spoke in sour verdicts sat to hand-crank
the tingling exchange, plugged us into each other's lives

and tapped consolation from gossip's cells as they unlidded.
From her shrewd kind successor who never tapped in, and planes
along below the eaves of our heads, we'll hear a tapestry
of weddings funerals surgeries, and after our sittings
be given a jar of pickle. Hers won't be like the house

a mile down the creek, where cards are cut and shuffled
in the middle of the day, and mortarbombs of beer
detonate the digestion, and they tell world-stopping yarns
like: I went to Sydney races. There along the rails,
all snap brims and cold eyes, flanked by senior police

and other, stony men with their eyes in a single crease
stood the entire Government of New South Wales
watching Darby ply the whip, all for show, over this fast colt.
It was young and naïve. It was heading for the post in a bolt
while the filly carrying his and all the inside money

strained to come level. Too quick for the stewards to note him
Darby slipped the colt a low lash to the scrotum.
It checked, shocked, stumbled – and the filly flashed by.
As he came from weighing in, I caught Darby's eye
and he said *Get out of it, mug,* quite conversationally.–

CAVE DIVERS NEAR MOUNT GAMBIER

Chenille-skinned people are counting under the countryside

on resurrections by truck light off among the pines.

Here in the first paddocks, where winter comes ashore,
mild duckweed ponds are skylights of a filled kingdom

and what their gaze absorbs may float up districts away.
White men with scorches of hair approach that water,

zip into black, upturn large flap feet and free-fall
away, their mouths crammed full. Crystalline polyps

of their breathing blossom for a while, as they disturb
algal screens, extinct kangaroos, eels of liquorice colour

then, with the portable greening stars they carry under,
these vanish, as the divers undergo tight anti-births

into the vaults and profound domes of the limestone.
Here, approaching the heart of the poem they embody

and thereby make the gliding cavern-world embody,
they have to keep time with themselves, and be dull often

with its daylight logic – since to dream it fully

might leave them asprawl on the void clang of their
tanks,

their faceplates glazing an unfocused dreadful portrait
at the apex of a steeple that does not reach the day.

THE BALLAD OF THE BARBED WIRE OCEAN

No more rice pudding. Pink coupons for Plume.
Smokes under the lap for aunts.
Four running black boots beside a red sun. Flash
wireless words like Advarnce.
When the ocean was wrapped in barbed wire, terror
radiant up the night sky,
exhilaration raced flat out in squadrons; Mum's
friends took off sun-hats to cry.

Starting south of the then world with new showground
rifles being screamed at and shown
for a giggle-suit three feeds a day and no more plans
of your own,
it went with some swagger till God bless you, Tom!
and Daddy come back! at the train
or a hoot up the gangways for all the girls and soon
the coast fading in rain,

but then it was flared screams from blood-bundles
whipped rolling as iron bombs keened down

and the insect-eyed bombers burned their crews alive
 in off-register henna and brown.
In steep ruins of rainforest pre-affluent thousands
 ape-scuttling mixed sewage with blood
and fear and the poem played vodka to morals, fear
 jolting to the mouth like cud.

It was sleep atop supplies, it was pickhandle, it was
 coming against the wall in tears,
sometimes it was factory banter, stoking jerked
 breechblocks and filing souvenirs,
or miles-wide humming cattleyards of humans, or
 oiled ship-fires slanting in ice,
rag-wearers burst as by huge War Bonds coins, girls'
 mouths full of living rice.

No one came home from it. Phantoms smoked two
 hundred daily. Ghosts held civilians at bay,
since war turns beyond strut and adventure to keeping
 what you've learned, and shown,
what you've approved, and what you've done, from
 ever reaching your own.
This is died for. And nihil and nonsense feed on it day
 after day.

THE TIN WASH DISH

Lank poverty, dank poverty,
its pants wear through at fork and knee.
It warms its hands over burning shames,

refers to its fate as Them and He
and delights in things by their hard names:
rag and toejam, feed and paw–
don't guts that down, there ain't no more!
Dank poverty, rank poverty,
it hums with a grim fidelity
like wood-rot with a hint of orifice,
wet newspaper jammed in the gaps of artifice,
and disgusts us into fierce loyalty.
It's never the fault of those you love:
poverty comes down from above.
Let it dance chairs and smash the door,
it arises from all that went before
and every outsider's the enemy–
Jesus Christ turned this over with his stick
and knights and philosophers turned it back.
Rank poverty, lank poverty,
chafe in its crotch and sores in its hair,
still a window's clean if it's made of air,
not webby silver like a sleeve.
Watch out if this does well at school
and has to leave and longs to leave:
someone, sometime, will have to pay.
Shave with toilet soap, run to flesh,
astound the nation, rule the army,
still you wait for the day you'll be sent back
where books or toys on the floor are rubbish
and no one's allowed to come and play
because home calls itself a shack
and hot water crinkles in the tin wash dish.

BATS' ULTRASOUND

Sleeping-bagged in a duplex wing
with fleas, in rock-cleft or building
radar bats are darkness in miniature,
their whole face one tufty crinkled ear
with weak eyes, fine teeth bared to sing.

Few are vampires. None flit through the mirror.
Where they flutter at evening's a queer
tonal hunting zone above highest C.
Insect prey at the peak of our hearing
drone re to their detailing tee:

ah, eyrie-ire, aero hour, eh?
O'er our ur-area (our era aye
ere your raw row) we air our array,
err, yaw, row wry – aura our orrery,
our eerie ü our ray, our arrow.

A rare ear, our aery Yahweh.

LYREBIRD

Liar made of leaf-litter, quivering ribby in shim,
hen-sized under froufrou, chinks in a quiff display him
or her, dancing in mating time, or out. And in any
order.
Tailed mimic aeon-sent to intrigue the next recorder,

I mew catbird, I saw crosscut, I howl she-dingo, I kink
forest hush distinct with bellbirds, warble magpie garble, link
cattlebell with kettle-boil; I rank ducks' cranky presidium
or simulate a triller like a rill mirrored lyrical to a rim.
I ring dim. I alter nothing. Real to real only I sing,
Gahn the crane to Gun the chainsaw, urban thing to being,
Screaming woman owl and human talk: eedieAi and uddyunnunoan.
The miming is all of I. Silent, they are a function
of wet forest, cometary lyrebirds. Their flight lifts them barely a semitone.

CATTLE ANCESTOR

Darrambawli and all his wives, they came feeding from the south east
back in that first time. Darrambawli is a big red fellow,
terrible fierce. He scrapes up dust, singing, whirling his bullroarers
in the air: he swings them and they sing out Crack! Crack!
All the time he's mounting his women, all the time more *kulka,*
more, more, smelling their *kulka* and looking down his nose.

Kangaroo and emu mobs run from him, as he tears up their shelters,
throwing the people in the air, stamping out their fires.
Darrambawli gathers up his brothers, all making that sad cry *mar mar:*
he initiates his brothers, the Bulluktruk. They walk head down in a line
and make the big blue ranges. You hear their clinking noise in there.
Darrambawli has wives everywhere, he has to gallop back and forth,
mad for their *kulka.* You see him on the coast, and on the plains.
They're eating up the country, so the animals come to spear them:
You have to die now, you're starving us. But then Waark the crow
tells Darrambawli Your wives, they're spearing them. He is screaming,
frothing at the mouth, that's why his chest is all white nowadays.
Jerking two knives, he screams *I make new waterholes! I bring the best song!*
He makes war on all that mob, raging, dotting the whole country.
He frightens the water-snakes; they run away, they can't sit down.
The animals forget how to speak. There is only one song

for a while. Darrambawli must sing it on his own.

THE OCTAVE OF ELEPHANTS

Bull elephants, when not weeping need, wander
 soberly alone.
Only females congregate and talk, in a seismic
 baritone:

Dawn and sundown we honour you, Jehovah Brahm,
who allow us to intone our ground bass in towering
 calm.

Inside the itchy fur of life is the sonorous planet
 Stone
which we hear and speak through, depending our
 flugelhorn.

Winds barrel, waves shunt shore, earth moans in
 ever-construction
being hurried up the sky, against weight, by endless
 suction.

We are two species, male and female. Bulls run to
 our call.
We converse. They weep, and announce, but rarely
 talk at all.

As presence resembles everything, our bulls reflect
 its solitude

and we, suckling, blaring, hotly loving, reflect its motherhood.

Burnt-maize-smelling Death, who brings the collapse-sound *bum-bum,*
has embryos of us on its free limbs: four legs and a thumb.

From dusting our newborn with puffs, we assume a boggling pool
into our heads, to re-silver each other's wrinkles and be cool.

THE COWS ON KILLING DAY

All me are standing on feed. The sky is shining.

All me have just been milked. Teats all tingling still
from that dry toothless sucking by the chilly mouths
that gasp loudly in in in, and never breathe out.

All me standing on feed, move the feed inside me.
One me smells of needing the bull, that heavy urgent me,
the back-climber, who leaves me humped, straining, but light
and peaceful again, with crystalline moving inside me.

Standing on wet rock, being milked, assuages the calf-sorrow in me.

Now the me who needs mounts on me, hopping, to signal the bull.

The tractor comes trotting in its grumble; the heifer human
bounces on top of it, and cud comes with the tractor,
big rolls of tight dry feed: lucerne, clovers, buttercup, grass,
that's been bitten but never swallowed, yet is cud.
She walks up over the tractor and down it comes, roll on roll
and all me following, eating it, and dropping the good pats.

The heifer human smells of needing the bull human
and is angry. All me look nervously at her
as she chases the dog me dream of horning dead: our enemy
of the light loose tongue. Me'd jam him in his squeals.

Me, facing every way, spreading out over feed.

One me is still in the yard, the place skinned of feed.
Me, old and sore-boned, little milk in that me now,
licks at the wood. The oldest bull human is coming.

Me in the peed yard. A stick goes out from the human
and cracks, like the whip. Me shivers and falls down
with the terrible, the blood of me, coming out behind an ear.

Me, that other me, down and dreaming in the bare yard.

All me come running. It's like the Hot Part of the sky
that's hard to look at, this that now happens behind wood
in the raw yard. A shining leaf, like off the bitter gum tree
is with the human. It works in the neck of me
and the terrible floods out, swamped and frothy. All me make the Roar,
some leaping stiff-kneed, trying to horn that worst horror.
The wolf-at-the-calves is the bull human. Horn the bull human!

But the dog and the heifer human drive away all me.

Looking back, the glistening leaf is still moving.
All of dry old me is crumpled, like the hills of feed,
and a slick me like a huge calf is coming out of me.

The carrion-stinking dog, who is calf of human and wolf,
is chasing and eating little blood things the humans scatter
and all me run away, over smells, toward the sky.

SPERMACETI

I sound my sight, and flexing skeletons eddy
in our common wall. With a sonic bolt from the fragrant
chamber of my head, I burst the lives of some
and slow, backwashing them into my mouth. I lighten,
breathe, and laze below again. And peer in long low tones
over the curve of Hard to river-tasting and oil-tasting
coasts, to the grand grinding coasts of rigid air.
How the wall of our medium has a shining, pumping rim:
the withstood crush of deep flight in it, perpetual entry!
Only the holes of eyesight and breath still tie us
to the dwarf-making Air, where true sight barely functions.
The power of our wall likewise guards us from
slowness of the rock Hard, its life-powdering compaction,
from its fissures and streamy layers that we sing into sight
but are silent, fixed, disjointed in. Eyesight is a leakage
of nearby into us, and shows us the tastes of food
conformed over its spines. But our greater sight is uttered.

I sing beyond the curve of distance the living joined bones
of my song-fellows; I sound a deep volcano's valve tubes
storming whitely in black weight; I receive an island's slump,
song-scrambling ship's heartbeats, and the sheer shear
of current-forms
bracketing a seamount. The wall, which running blind I demolish,
heals, prickling me with sonars. My every long shaped cry
re-establishes the world, and centres its ringing structure.

THE WEDDING AT BERRICO

Christina and James, 8th February 1992

To reach your watershed country
we've driven this summer's green climbs
and the creekwater film spooling over
causeways got spliced many times
with its boulders like ice under whisky,
tree pools mirrory as the eyes of horses.
Great hills above, the house *en fête:*
we've parked between soaring rhymes
and slipped in among brilliant company.

Here are your gifts. I see God's sent
all your encounters so far with him:
life. Landscape. Unfraught love. Some poetry.
Risk too, with his star rigger Freedom,
but here's poise, for whatever may come.
What's life wish you? Sound genetics, delight,
long resilience against gravity, the sight
of great-grandchildren, a joint sense of home.

Hey, all these wishes in smart boxes! Fun,
challenges, Meaning, work-satisfaction–
this must be the secular human lot: health
till high old age, children of character,
dear friendships. And the testing one: wealth.
Quietly we add ours: may you
always have each other, and want to.

Few poems I've made mention our children.
That I write at all got you dork names.
More might have brought worse. Our jealous nation...
I am awed at you, though, today,
silk restraining your briskness and gumption,
my mother's face still hauntingly in yours

and this increase, this vulnerable beauty.
James is worthy of his welcome to our family.
Never would I do, or he ask
me to do what no parental memories
could either: I won't give you away.

But now you join hands, exchanging
the vows that cost joyfully dear.
They move you to the centre of life
and us gently to the rear.

DEAD TREES IN THE DAM

Castle scaffolding tall in moat,
the dead trees in the dam
flower each morning with birds.

It can be just the three resident
cormorants with musket-hammer necks, plus
the clinician spoonbill, its long pout;

twilight's herons who were almost too lightfoot
to land; pearl galahs in pink-fronted
confederacy, each starring in its frame,

or it may be a misty candelabrum
of egrets lambent before saint Sleep–
who gutter awake and balance stiffly off.

Odd mornings, it's been all bloodflag
and rifle green: a stopped-motion shrapnel
of kingparrots. Smithereens when they freaked.

Rarely, it's wed ducks, whose children
will float among the pillars. In daytime
magpies sidestep up wood to jag pinnacles

and the big blow-in cuckoo crying
Alarm, Alarm on the wing is not let light.
This hours after dynastic charts of high

profile ibis have rowed away to beat
the paddocks. Which, however green, are
always watercolour, and on brown paper.

LATE SUMMER FIRES

The paddocks shave black
with a foam of smoke that stays,
welling out of red-black wounds.

In the white of a drought
this happens. The hardcourt game.
Logs that fume are mostly cattle,

inverted, stubby. Tree stumps are kilns.
Walloped, wiped, hand-pumped,
even this day rolls over, slowly.

At dusk, a family drives sheep
out through the yellow
of the Aboriginal flag.

CORNICHE

I work all day and hardly drink at all.

I can reach down and feel if I'm depressed.
I adore the Creator because I made myself
and a few times a week a wire jags in my chest.

The first time, I'd been coming apart all year,
weeping, incoherent; cigars had given me up;
any road round a cliff edge I'd whimper along in low gear
then: cardiac horror. Masking my pulse's calm lub-dup.

It was the victim-sickness. Adrenalin howling in my head,
the black dog was my brain. Come to drown me in my breath
was energy's black hole, depression, compère of the predawn show
when, returned from a pee, you stew and welter in your death.

The rogue space rock is on course to snuff your world,
sure. But go acute, and its oncoming fills your day.
The brave die but once? I could go a hundred times a week,
clinging to my pulse with the world's edge inches away.

Laugh, who never shrank around wizened genitals there
or killed themselves to stop dying. The blow that never falls

batters you stupid. Only gradually do
you notice a slight scorn in you for what appals.

A self inside self, cool as conscience, one to be erased
in your final night, or faxed, still knows beneath
all the mute grand opera and uncaused effect–
that death which can be imagined is not true death.

The crunch is illusion. There's still no outside world
but you start to see. You're like one enthralled by bad
 art–
yet for a real onset, what cover! You gibber to
 Casualty,
are checked, scorned, calmed. There's nothing wrong
 with your heart.

The terror of death is not afraid of death.
Fear, pure, is intransitive. A Hindenburg of vast rage
rots, though, above your life. See it, and you feel
 flogged
but like an addict you sniffle aboard, to your cage,

because you will cling to this beast as it gnaws you,
for the crystal in its kidneys, the elixir in its wings,
till your darlings are the police of an immense fatigue.
I came to the world unrehearsed but I've learned
 some things.

When you curl, stuffed, in the pot at rainbow's end
it is life roaring and racing and nothing you can do.

Were you really God you could have lived all the
 lives
that now decay into misery and cripple you.

A for adrenalin, the original A-bomb, fuel
and punishment of aspiration, the Enlightenment's
 air-burst.
Back when God made me, I had no script. It was
 better.
For all the death, we also die unrehearsed.

LIKE WHEELING STACKED WATER

Dried nests in the overhanging limbs
are where the flood hatched eggs of swirl.
Like is unscary milder love. More can be in it.

The flood boomed up nearly to the door
like a taxiing airliner. It flew past all day.
Now the creek is down to barley colour
waist deep on her, chest on him,
wearing glasses all around them, barely pushing.

Down under stops of deadwood pipe in living
branches, they move on again. The bottom
is the sunk sand cattle-road they know
but hidden down cool, and mincing
magically away at every step, still going.

The wide creek is a tree hall decorated

with drowned and tobacco ribbons,
with zippy tilting birds, with dried snakes hanging
over the doorways everywhere along.

They push on. *Say this log I'm walking
under the water's a mast like off a
olden day ship–.* Fine hessian shade
is moistening down off cross-trees,

and like wings, the rocking waterline
gloving up and down their bodies
pumps support to their swimmy planet steps.

They've got a hook and bits
of bluebottle line from salt holidays.
They had a poor worm, and crickets automatic in a
 jar
but they let all them off fishing.

They're taking like to an adventure instead, up past there where the undercut bank makes that bottling noise, and the kingfisher's beak is like the weight he's thrown by to fly him straight.

By here, they're wheeling stacked-up water. It has mounted like mild ice bedclothes to their chest and chin. They have to tiptoe under all the white davits of the bush.

But coming to the island, that is like the pupil in acres of eye, their clothes pour water off like heavy chain. They toil, and lighten as they go up on it. All this is like the past but none of it is sad. It has never ended.

IT ALLOWS A PORTRAIT IN LINE SCAN AT FIFTEEN

He retains a slight 'Martian' accent, from the years of single phrases.

He no longer hugs to disarm. It is gradually allowing him affection.

It does not allow proportion. Distress is absolute, shrieking, and runs him at frantic speed through crashing doors.

He likes cyborgs. Their taciturn power, with his intonation.

It still runs him around the house, alone in the dark, cooing and laughing.

He can read about soils, populations and New Zealand. On neutral topics he's illiterate.

Arnie Schwarzenegger is an actor. He isn't a cyborg really, is he, Dad?

He lives on forty acres, with animals and trees, and used to draw it continually.

He knows the map of Earth's fertile soils, and can draw it freehand.

He can only lie in a panicked shout *SorrySorryI-didn'tdoit!* warding off conflict with others and himself.

When he ran away constantly it was to the greengrocers to worship stacked fruit.

His favourite country was the Ukraine: it is nearly all deep fertile soil.

Giggling, he climbed all over the dim Freudian psychiatrist who told us how autism resulted from 'refrigerator' parents.

When asked to smile, he photographs a rictus-smile on his face.

It long forbade all naturalistic films. They were Adult movies.

If they (that is, he) *are bad the police will put them in hospital.*

He sometimes drew the farm amid Chinese or Balinese rice terraces.

When a runaway, he made uproar in the police station, playing at three times adult speed.

Only animated films were proper. *Who Framed Roger Rabbit* then authorised the rest.

Phrases spoken to him he would take as teaching, and repeat.

When he worshipped fruit, he screamed as if poisoned when it was fed to him.

A one-word first conversation: *Blane. – Yes! Plane, that's right, baby! – Blane.*

He has forgotten nothing, and remembers the precise quality of experiences.

It requires rulings: Is *stealing very playing up, as bad as murder?*

He counts at a glance, not looking. And he has never been lost.

When he ate only nuts and dried fruit, words were for dire emergencies.
He knows all the breeds of fowls, and the counties of Ireland.
He'd begun to talk, then returned to babble, then silence. It withdrew speech for years.
When he took your hand, it was to work it, as a multipurpose tool.
He is anger's mirror, and magnifies any near him, raging it down.
It still won't allow him fresh fruit, or orange juice with bits in it.
He swam in the midwinter dam at night. It had no rules about cold.
He was terrified of thunder and finally cried as if in explanation It – *angry!*
He grilled an egg he'd broken into bread. Exchanges of soil-knowledge are called landtalking.
He lives in objectivity. I was sure Bell's palsy would leave my face only when he said it had begun to.
Don't say word! when he was eight forbade the word 'autistic' in his presence.
Bantering questions about girlfriends cause a terrified look and blocked ears.
He sometimes centred the farm in a furrowed American Midwest.
Eye contact, Mum! means he truly wants attention. It dislikes I-contact.
He is equitable and kind, and only ever a little jealous. It was a relief when that little arrived.

He surfs, bowls, walks for miles. For many years he hasn't trailed his left arm while running.
I gotta get smart! looking terrified into the years. *I gotta get smart!*

THE SHIELD-SCALES OF HERALDRY

Surmounting my government's high evasions
stands a barbecue of crosses and birds
tended by a kangaroo and emu
but in our courts, above the judge,
a lion and a unicorn still keep
their smaller offspring, plus a harp,
in an open prison looped with mottoes.

Coats of arms, plaster Rorschach blots,
crowned stone moths, they encrust Europe.
As God was dismissed from churches
they fluttered in and cling to the walls,
abstract comic-pages held by scrolled beasts,
or wear on the flagstones underfoot.
They pertain to an earlier Antichrist,

the one before police. Mafiose citadels
made them, states of one attended family
islanded in furrows. The oldest
are the simplest. A cross, some coins,
a stripe, a roof tree, a spur rowel,
bowstaves, a hollow-gutted lion,
and all in lucid target colours.

Under tinned heads with reveries tied on,
shields are quartered and cubed by marriage
till they are sacred campaign maps
or anatomy inside dissected mantling,
glyphs minutely clear through their one
rule, that colour must abut either
gold or silver, the non-weapon metals.

The New World doesn't blazon well–
the new world ran away from blazonry
or was sent away in chains by it–
but exceptions shine: the spread eagle
with the fireworks display on its belly
and in the thinks-balloon above its head.
And when as a half-autistic

kid in scrub paddocks vert and or
I grooved on the cloisons of pedigree
it was a vivid writing of system
that hypnotised me, beyond the obvious
euphemism of force. It was eight hundred
years of cubist art and Europe's dreamings:
the Cup, the Rose, the Ship, the Antlers.

High courage, bestial snobbery,
neither now merits ungrace from us.
They could no longer hang me,
throttling, for a rabbit sejant.
Like everyone, I would now be lord
or lady myself, and pardon me

or myself loose the coronet-necked hounds.

BURNING WANT

From just on puberty, I lived in funeral:
mother dead of miscarriage, father trying to be dead,
we'd boil sweat-brown cloth; cows repossessed the
 garden.
Lovemaking brought death, was the unuttered
 principle.

I met a tall adopted girl some kids thought aloof,
but she was intelligent. Her poise of white-blonde hair
proved her no kin to the squat tanned couple who
 loved her.
Only now do I realise she was my first love.

But all my names were fat-names, at my new town
 school.
Between classes, kids did erocide: destruction of
 sexual morale.
Mass refusal of unasked love; that works. Boys
 cheered as seventeen-year-old
girls came on to me, then ran back whinnying ridicule.

The slender girl came up on holidays from the city
to my cousins' farm. She was friendly and sane.
Whispers giggled round us. A letter was written as
 from me
and she was there, in mid-term, instantly.

But I called people 'the humans' not knowing it was rage.
I learned things sidelong, taking my rifle for walks,
recited every scene of *From Here to Eternity,* burned paddocks
and soldiered back each Monday to that dawning Teen age.

She I admired, and almost relaxed from placating,
was gnawed by knowing what she came from, not who.
Showing off was my one social skill, oddly never with her
but I dissembled feelings, till mine were unknown to me too

and I couldn't add my want to her shortfall of wantedness.
I had forty more years, with one dear remission,
of a white paralysis: she's attracted it's not real nothing is enough
she's mistaken she'll die go now! she'll tell any minute she'll laugh–

Whether other hands reached out to Marion, or didn't,
at nineteen in her training ward she had a fatal accident
alone, at night, they said, with a lethal injection
and was spared from seeing what my school did to the world.

THE LAST HELLOS

Don't die, Dad–
but they die.

This last year he was wandery:
took off a new chainsaw blade
and cobbled a spare from bits.
Perhaps if I lay down
my head'll come better again.
His left shoulder kept rising
higher in his cardigan.

He could see death in a face.
Family used to call him in
to look at sick ones and say.
At his own time, he was told.

The knob found in his head
was duck-egg size. Never hurt.
Two to six months, Cecil.

I'll be right, he boomed
to his poor sister on the phone
I'll do that when I finish dyin.

***

Don't die, Cecil.
But they do.

Going for last drives
in the bush, odd massive
board-slotted stumps bony white
in whipstick second growth.
I could chop all day.

I could always cash
a cheque, in Sydney or anywhere.
Any of the shops.

Eating, still at the head
of the table, he now missed
food on his knife side.

Sorry, Dad, but like
have you forgiven your enemies?
Your father and all them?
All his lifetime of hurt.

I must have (grin). *I don't*
think about that now.

***

People can't say goodbye
any more. They say last hellos.

Going fast, over Christmas,
he'd still stumble out
of his room, where his photos

hang over the other furniture,
and play host to his mourners.

The courage of his bluster
firm big voice of his confusion.

Two last days in the hospital:
his long forearms were still
red mahogany. His hands
gripped steel frame. *I'm dyin.*

On the second day:
You're bustin to talk but
I'm too busy dyin.

***

Grief ended when he died,
the widower like soldiers who
won't live life their mates missed.

Good boy Cecil! No more Bluey dog.
No more cowtime. No more stories.
We're still using your imagination,
it was stronger than all ours.

Your grave's got littler
somehow, in the three months.
More pointy as the clay's srivelled,
like a stuck zip in a coat.

Your cricket boots are in
the State museum! Odd letters
still come. Two more's died since you:
Annie, and Stewart. Old Stewart.

On your day there was a good crowd,
family, and people from away.
But of course a lot had gone
to their own funerals first.

Snobs mind us off religion
nowadays, if they can.
Fuck thém. I wish you God.

COTTON FLANNELETTE

Shake the bed, the blackened child whimpers,
O shake the bed! through beak lips that never
will come unwry. And wearily the ironframed
mattress, with nodding crockery bulbs,
jinks on its way.

Her brothers and sister take
shifts with the terrible glued-together baby
when their unsleeping absolute mother
reels out to snatch an hour, back to stop
the rocking and wring pale blue soap-water
over nude bladders and blood-webbed chars.

Even their cranky evasive father

is awed to stand watches rocking the bed.
Lids frogged shut, *O please shake the bed,*
her contour whorls and braille tattoos
from where, in her nightdress, she flared
out of hearth-drowse to a marrow shriek
pedalling full tilt firesleeves in mid air,

are grainier with repair
than when the doctor, crying *Dear God, woman!*
No one can save that child. Let her go!
spared her the treatments of the day.

Shake the bed. Like: count phone poles, rhyme,
classify realities, bang the head, any
iteration that will bring, in the brain's forks,
the melting molecules of relief,
and bring them again.

O rock the bed!
Nibble water with bared teeth, make lymph
like arrowroot gruel, as your mother grips you
for weeks in the untrained perfect language,
till the doctor relents. Salves and wraps you
in dressings that will be the fire again,
ripping anguish off agony,

and will confirm
the ploughland ridges the gum joins
in your woman's skin, child saved by rhythm
for the sixty more years your family weaves you

on devotion's loom, rick-racking the bed
as you yourself, six years old, instruct them.

THE HARLEYS

Blats booted to blatant
dubbin the avenue dire
with rubbings of Sveinn Forkbeard
leading a black squall of Harleys
with Moe Snow-Whitebeard and

Possum Brushbeard and their ladies
and, sphincter-lipped, gunning,
massed leather muscle on a run,
on a roll, Santas from Hell
like a whole shoal leaning

wide-wristed, their tautness stable
in fluency, fast streetscape dwindling,
all riding astride, on the outside
of sleek grunt vehicles, woman-clung,
forty years on from Marlon.

DREAMBABWE

Streaming, a hippo surfaces
like the head of someone
lifting, with still entranced eyes,
from a lake of stanzas.

THE INSTRUMENT

Who reads poetry? Not our intellectuals;
they want to control it. Not lovers, not the combative,
not examinees. They too skim it for bouquets
and magic trump cards. Not poor schoolkids
furtively farting as they get immunized against it.

Poetry is read by the lovers of poetry
and heard by some more they coax to the cafe
or the district library for a bifocal reading.
Lovers of poetry may total a million people
on the whole planet. Fewer than the players of *skat.*

What gives them delight is a never-murderous skim
distilled, to verse mainly, and suspended in rapt
calm on the surface of paper. The rest of poetry
to which this was once integral still rules
the continents, as it always did. But on condition now

that its true name is never spoken: constructs, feral poetry,
the opposite but also the secret of the rational.
And who reads that? Ah, the lovers, the schoolkids,
debaters, generals, crime-lords, everybody reads it:
Porsche, lift-off, Gaia, Cool, patriarchy.

Among the feral stanzas are many that demand your flesh
to embody themselves. Only completed art
free of obedience to its time can pirouette you
through and athwart the larger poems you are in.
Being outside all poetry is an unreachable void.

Why write poetry? For the weird unemployment.
For the painless headaches, that must be tapped to strike
down along your writing arm at the accumulated moment.
For the adjustments after, aligning facets in a verb
before the trance leaves you. For working always beyond

your own intelligence. For not needing to rise
and betray the poor to do it. For a non-devouring fame.
Little in politics resembles it: perhaps
the Australian colonists' re-inventing of the snide
far-adopted secret ballot, in which deflation could hide

and, as a welfare bringer, shame the mass-grave Revolutions,
so axe-edged, so lictor-y.
Was that moral cowardice's one shining world victory?
Breathing in dream-rhythm when awake and far from bed

evinces the gift. Being tragic with a book on your head.

A DEPLOYMENT OF FASHION

In Australia, a lone woman
is being crucified by the Press
at any given moment.

With no unedited right
of reply, she is cast out
into Aboriginal space.

It's always for a defect in weeping:
she hasn't wept on cue
or she won't weep correctly.

There's a moment when the sharks are
still butting her, testing her protection,
when the Labor Party, or influence,

can still save her. Not the Church,
not other parties. Even at that stage
few men can rescue her.

Then she goes down, overwhelmed
in the feasting grins of pressmen,
and Press women who've moved

from being owned by men

to being owned by fashion,
these are more deeply merciless.

She is rogue property,
she must be taught her weeping.
It is done for the millions.

Sometimes the millions join in
with jokes: how to get a baby
in the Northern Territory? Just stick

your finger down a dingo's throat.
Most times, though, the millions
stay money, and the jokes

are snobbish media jokes:
Chemidenko. The Oxleymoron.
Spittle, like the flies on Black Mary.

After the feeding frenzy
sometimes a ruefully balanced last lick
precedes the next selection.

A POSTCARD

A mirrory tar-top road across
a wide plain. Drizzling sky.
A bike is parked at a large book
turned down tent-fashion on the verge.
One emerging says *I read such crazy*

things in this book. 'Every bird
has stone false teeth and enters
the world in its coffin.' That's in there.

DOWNHILL ON BORROWED SKIS

White mongrel I hate snow
wadded numbing mousse
grog face in a fur noose
the odd miraculous view
through glass or killing you
the only time I skied
I followed no skilled lead
but on parallel lent boards
fell straight down a hill
fell standing up by clenched will
very fast on toe-point swords
over logshapes and schist
outcrips crops it was no piste
nor had I had any drinks
wishing my ankles steel links
winging it hammer and Shazam
no stocks in afternoon mirk
every cloud-gap royally flash
like heading into a car crash
ayyy the pain! the paperwork!
my hands I didn't flail them
though neither left nor right
neither schuss nor slalom
my splitting splay twinned sled

pumping straining to spread
to a biplane wreck of snapped ligaments
all hell played with locked joints
but still I skidded down erect
in my long spill of grist
blinded hawk on a wrist
entirely unschooled unchecked
the worst going on not and not
happening no sprawl no bone-shot
till I stood on the flat
being unlatched and exclaimed at.

SOUND BITES

Attended by thousands, the Sun is opening

***

it's a body-prayer, a shower: you're
in touch all over, renewing, enfolded in a wing–

***

My sorrow, only ninety-five thousand
welcomes left in Scots Gaeldom now.

***

Poor cultures can afford poetry, wealthy cultures can't.

***

Sex is the ever-appeased class
system that defeats Utopias...

***

but I bask in the pink that you're in (Repeat)

***

one day, as two continents are dividing
the whole length of a river turns salt.

***

What's sketched at light speed
thunder must track, bumbling, for miles

***

If love shows you its terrible face
before its beautiful face, you'll be punished.

***

People watching with their mouths
an increasing sky-birth of meteors

***

Y chromosomes of history, apologise to your Xes!

THE IMAGES ALONE

Scarlet as the cloth draped over a sword,
white as steaming rice, blue as leschenaultia,
old curried towns, the frog in its green human skin;
a ploughman walking his furrow as if in irons, but
as at a whoop of young men running loose
in brick passages, there occurred the thought
like instant stitches all through crumpled silk:

as if he'd had to leap to catch the bullet.

A stench like hands out of the ground.
The willows had like beads in their hair, and
Peenemünde, grunted the dentist's drill, Peenemünde!
Fowls went on typing on every corn key, green
kept crowding the pinks of peach trees into the sky
but used speech balloons were tacky in the river
and waterbirds had liftoff as at a repeal of gravity.

ROOMS OF THE SKETCH-GARDEN

for Peter and Christine Alexander

Women made the gardens, in my world,
cottage style full-sun fanfares
netting-fenced, of tablecloth colours.

Shade is what I first tried to grow
one fence in from jealous pasture,
shade, which cattle rogueing into

or let into, could devour
and not hurt much. Shelter from glare
it rests their big eyes, and rests in them.

A graphite-toned background of air
it features red, focusses yellow.
Blue diffusing through it rings the firebell.

Shade makes colours loom and be thoughtful.
It has the afterlife atmosphere
but also the philosophic stone cool.

It is both day and night civilised,
the colour of reading, the tone
of inside, and of inside the mind.

I could call these four acres Hanlin
for the Chinese things they have nourished,
loquat, elm, mulberry, the hard pear

er ben lai. But other names would fit: Klagenfurt,
Moaner's Crossing, for the many things that die,
for worn-out farm soil, for the fruit fly.

Cloud shadows walking our pencilled roof
in summer sound like a feasting chook

or Kukukuku on about duk-duk

and this sketch garden's a retina for chance:
for floodwaters backing into the lower
parterres like lorryloads of mercury

at night, or level sepia by day,
for the twenty-three sorts of native vines
along the gully; for the heron-brought

igniting propane-blue waterlily,
for the white poplars' underworld advance
on the whole earth, out of my ignorance.

Tall Australians stand east of the house
and well north. The garden's not nationalist:
Australians burn, on winds from the west.

No birds that skim-drink, or bow
or flower in our spaces are owned now.
Jojo burrs make me skid my feet on lawn

being wary of long grass, like any bushman.
Begged and scavenged plants survived dry spells
best, back when I'd to garden in absentia:

Dad wouldn't grow flowers, or water ornamentals.
He mounded for the Iroquois three sisters,
corn beans and squash. And melons, and
 tomatoes.

Those years we'd plant our live Christmas tree
in January when it shed its brittle bells
and the drought sun bore down like dementia.

Now bloom-beds displace fox-ripped rooster
 plumes
in from paddocks, in our cattle-policed laager;
trampled weeds make wharves for the indigo
 waterhen.

OASIS CITY

Rose-red city in the angles of a cut-up
green anthology: grape stanzas, citrus strophes,
I like your dirt cliffs and chimney-broom palm
 trees,

your pipe dream under dust, in its heads of
 pressure.
I enjoy your landscape blown from the Pleistocene
and roofed in stick forests of tarmacadam blue.

Your river waltzed round thousands of loops to
 you
and never guessed. Now it's locked in a Grand
 Canal,
aerated with paddlewheels, feeder of kicking
 sprays,

its willows placid as geese outspread over young

or banner-streamed under flood. Hey, rose-red city
of the tragic fountain, of the expensive brink,

of crescent clubs, of flags basil-white-and-tomato,
I love how you were invented and turned on:
t he city as equipment, unpacking its intersections.

City dreamed wrongly true in Puglia and Antakya
with your unemployed orange-trunks globalised out
of the ground,
I delight in the mountains your flat scrub calls to
mind

and how you'd stack up if decanted over steep relief.
I praise your camel-train skies and tanglefoot
red-gums
and how you mine water, speed it to chrome lace
and slow it

to culture's ingredients. How you learn your
tolerance
on hideous pans far out, by the crystals of land
sweat.
Along high-speed vistas, action breaks out of you,

but sweeter are its arrivals back inside
dust-walls of evergreen, air watered with raisins and
weddings,
the beer of day pickers, the crash wine of night
pickers.

THE MOON MAN

Shadowy kangaroos moved off
as we drove into the top paddock
coming home from a wedding
under a midnightish curd sky

then his full face cleared:
Moon man, the first birth ever
who still massages his mother
and sends her light, for his having

been born fully grown.
His brilliance is in our blood.
Had Earth fully healed from that labour
no small births could have happened.

VISITOR

He knocks at the door
and listens to his heart approaching.

CLOTHING AS DWELLING AS SHOULDERED BOAT

Propped sheets of bark converging
over skin-oils and a winter fire,
stitched hides of a furry rug-cloak

with their naked backs to the weather,
clothing as dwelling as shouldered boat
beetle-backed, with bending ridgelines,
all this, resurrected and gigantic:
the Opera House,
Sydney's Aboriginal building.

JELLYFISH

Globe globe globe globe
soft glass bowls upside down
over serves of nutty udder and teats
under the surface of the sun.

A COUNTRYMAN

On the long flats north of the river
an elder in a leather jacket
is hitchhiking to his daughter's funeral.

IN A TIME OF CUISINE

A fact the gourmet
euphemism can't silence:
vegetarians eat sex,
carnivores eat violence.

THE CLIMAX OF FACTORY FARMING

Farm gates were sealed with tape;
people couldn't stop shaking their heads.
Out on the fells and low fields
in twilight, it was the Satanic mills
come again: the farm beasts of Britain
being burnt inside walls of their feed.

THE POISONS OF RIGHT AND LEFT

You are what you have got
and: to love, you have to hate.
Two ideas that have killed and maimed
holocausts and myriads.

TO ONE OUTSIDE THE CULTURE

Still ask me about adult stuff
when you want. But remember that day
in Madame Tussaud's basement
when all the grownups looked careful
and some young ones had to smirk?

You were right to cry out in horror
at the cut-off heads there
and the rusty dried trickles
shocked out of their eyes and ears.

THE MEANING OF EXISTENCE

Everything except language
knows the meaning of existence.
Trees, planets, rivers, time
know nothing else. They express it
moment by moment as the universe.

Even this fool of a body
lives it in part, and would
have full dignity within it
but for the ignorant freedom
of my talking mind.

THE HANGING GARDENS

High on the Gloucester road
just before it wriggles its hips
level with eagles down the gorge
into the coastal hills

there were five beige pea-chickens
sloping under the farm fence
in a nervous unison of head-tufts
up to the garden where they lived

then along the gutter and bank
adult birds, grazing in full serpent.
Their colours are too saturate and cool
to see at first with dryland eyes

trained to drab and ginger. No one here
believes in green deeply enough. In greens
so blue, so malachite. Animal cobalt too
and arrow bustles, those are unparalleled.

The wail lingers, and their cane
surrection of iridium plaques. Great spirits,
Hindoostan in the palette of New Zealand!
They don’t succeed at feral.

Things rush them from dry grass.
Haggard teeth climb to them. World birds,
human birds, flown by their own volition
they led us to palaces.

THE AVERTED

The one whose eyes
do not meet yours
is alone at heart
and looks where the dead look
for an ally in his cause.

PERCEPTS

Lying back so smugly
phallic, the ampersand
in the deckchair of itself.

***

The best love poems are known
as such to the lovers alone.

***

Tired from understanding
life, the animals approach man
to be mystified.

***

Filling in a form
the simple man asks his mother
Mum, what sex are we?

TRAVELLING THE BRITISH ROADS

Climb out of mediaeval one-way
and roundabouts make knotted rope
of the minor British roads
but legal top speed on the rocketing
nickel motorway is a lower limit!
I do it, and lorries howl past me.

Sometimes after brown food
at a pub, I get so slow
that Highland trackways
only have one side

since they are for feet
and hoofs of pack horses
and passing is ceremony.

Nor is it plovers
which cry in the peopled glens
but General Wade's chainmen
shouting numbers for his road
not in the Gaelic scores
but in decimal English.

Universal roads return as shoal
late in the age of iron rims.
Stones in the top layer to be
no bigger than would fit in your mouth,
smiles John McAdam. *If in doubt*
test them with your lips!

Highwaymen, used to reining in
thoroughbreds along a quag of track,
suddenly hang, along new carriageways
or clink iron on needy slave-ships,
but wagon horses start surviving
seven years instead of three
at haulage between new smoke towns.

Then railways silence the white road.
A horseman rides alone between villages;
the odd gig, or phaeton;
smoke and music of the *bosh*

rising out of chestnut shade:
Gypsies, having a heyday.
Post roads, drying out, seem strange
beaches, that intersect each other.

When housemaids uncovered their hair
at windows, and a newfangled
steam roller made seersucker sounds
there were swans on the healed canal,
and with the sun came the Queen's
Horse Artillery in tight skeleton coats
to exercise their dubbined teams
watched by both fashionable sexes
in bloomer-like pedal pants.

I knew to be wary of the best dressed,
decent with the footsore,
but frontier-raffish with all
because the scripts they improvised from
were dry and arch, but quickly earnest.

From that day, and the audible
woodwind cry of peafowl, it was half
a long lifetime till jerked motors
would ripple the highroad
with their soundwaves, like a palate,
and kiss its gravel out
with round rubber lips
growling for the buckets of tar

and another life to the autobahn
nothing joins, where I race the mirror
in a fighter cockpit made posh
under flak of Guy Fawkes eve
over the cities of fumed brick.

FOR AN EIGHTIETH BIRTHDAY

i. m. Lewis Deer

On a summer morning after the war
you're walking with the Belle of the Ball
both in your new pressed sports gear
over grass towards the scotching sound
of tennis balls on lined antbed
inside the netting's tall swarm.

You glance past the wartime rifle range
below the great cattle hill
that lifts your family name high
and into the gap the Japanese
soldiers never reached, there where
your years of farming will happen.

Bounce comes in your step from strung
racquets, from neighbours still young,
from unnoticed good of sun and birds
and the understandings calmly dancing
between you two, walking into the stroke-play
of gee-ups on a tournament Saturday.

BLACK BELT IN MARITAL ARTS

Pork hock and jellyfish. Poor cock.
King Henry had a marital block.
A dog in the manager? Don't mock!
denial flows past Cairo.

A rhyme is a pun that knows where
to stop. Puns pique us with the glare
of worlds too coherent to bear
by any groan person.

Nothing moved him like her before.
It was like hymn and herbivore,
Serbs some are too acerbic for–
punning moves toward music.

A LEVITATION OF LAND

October 2002

Haze went from smoke-blue to beige
gradually, after midday.
The Inland was passing over
high up, and between the trees.

The north hills and the south hills
lost focus and faded away.

As the Inland was passing over

lungless flies quizzing road kill
got clogged with aerial plaster.
Familiar roads ended in vertical
paddocks unfenced in abstraction.
The sun was back to animating clay.

The whole ploughed fertile crescent
inside the ranges' long bow
offered up billion-tonne cargo
compound of hoofprints and debt,
stark street vistas, diesel and sweat.
This finest skim of drought particles

formed a lens, fuzzy with grind,
a shield the length of Northern Europe
and had the lift of a wing
which traffic of thermals kept amassing
over the mountains. Grist the shade
of kitchen blinds sprinkled every scene.

A dustbowl inverted in the sky
shared the coast out in bush-airfield sizes.
A surfer from the hundred acre sea
landed on the beach's narrow squeak
and re-made his home town out of pastry.
A sense of brown snake in the air

and dogs whiffed, scanning their nosepaper.
Teenagers in the tan foreshortening
regained, for moments, their child voices,

and in double image, Vanuatu to New Zealand
an echo-Australia gathered out on the ocean
having once more scattered itself from its urn.

ON THE NORTH COAST LINE

The train coming on up the Coast
fitting like a snake into water
is fleeing the sacrificial crust
of suburbs built into fire forest.
Today, smoke towers above there.

We've winged along sills of the sea
we've traversed the Welsh and Geordie
placenames where pickaxe coughing
won coal from miners' crystal lungs.
No one aboard looks wealthy:

wives, non-drivers, Aborigines,
sun-crackled workers. The style
of country trains isn't lifestyle.
River levees round old chain-gang towns
fall away behind our run of windows.

By cuttings like hangars filled with rock
to Stroud Road, and Stratford on the Avon,
both named by Robert Dawson, who ordered
convicts hung for drowning Native children
but the Governor stopped him. God

help especially the underdogs of underdogs
and the country now is spread hide
harnessed with sparse human things
and miles ahead, dawning into mind
under its approaching cobalt-inked

Chinese scroll of drapefold mountains
waits Dawson's homesick Gloucester
where Catholics weren't allowed to live.
There people crowd out onto the platform
to blow smoke like a regiment, before windows

carry them on, as ivory phantoms
who might not quip, or sue,
between the haunches of the hills
where the pioneer Isabella Mary Kelly
(She poisons flour! Sleeps with bushrangers!

She flogs her convicts herself!)
refusing any man's protection
rode with pocket pistols. Which
on this coast, made her the Kelly
whom slander forced to bear the whole guilt,

when it was real, of European settlement.
Now her name gets misremembered:
Kelly's crossing, Kate Kelly's Crossing
and few battlers on this train
think they live in a European settlement

and on a platform down the first
subtropic river, patched velvet girls
get met by their mothers' lovers,
lawn bowlers step down clutching their nuclei
and a walking frame is hoisted yea! like swords.

THE NOSTRIL SONGS

P. Ovidius Naso
when banished from Rome
remained in the city
for days on slave clothing,
for weeks in his study,
for decades in living noses–

***

Trees register the dog

and the dog receives the forest
as it trots toward the trees

then the sleeping tiger
reaches the dog en masse
before the dog reaches the tiger:
this from the Bengal forests
in the upper Kerosene age,

curry finger-lines in shock fur.

***

The woman in the scarlet tapestry
who stands up on a sprigged cushion
of land in space, is in fact
nude, as all are in the nostril-world.

What seem to be her rich gowns
are quotations from plants and animals
modulating her tucked, demure
but central olfactory heart

and her absent lover, pivoting
on his smaller salt heart
floats banner-like above her.

***

No stench is infra dog.

***

Fragrance stays measured,
stench bloats out of proportion:
even a rat-sized death,
not in contact with soil, is soon
a house-evacuating metal gas
in our sinuses; it boggles our gorge.
No saving that sofa:
give it a Viking funeral!

***

The kingdom of ghosts
has two nostril doors
like the McDonald's symbol.

You are summoned to breathe
the air of another time
that is home, that is desperate,
the tinctures, the sachets.

You yourself are a ghost.
If you were there
you are still there–

even if you're alive
out in the world of joking.

For other species, the nasal kingdom
is as enslaved and barbed
as the urine stars around all territory,

as the coke lines of autumn
snorting into a truffle-pig's head

or the nose-gaffed stallion,
still an earner, who screams rising
for the tenth time in a day.

***

Mammal self-portraits
are everywhere, rubbed on
or sprayed on in an instant.

Read by nose, they don't give
the outline shapes demanded
by that wingless bird the human;

with our beak and eyes
we perceive them as smears
or turds, or nothing at all.

Painted from inside
these portraits give the inner
truth of their subject

with no reserve or lie.
Warned or comforted or stirred
every mammal's an unfoolable

connoisseur, with its fluids
primed to judge, as it moves
through an endless exhibition.

***

Half the reason for streets,
they're to walk in the buzz
the sexes find vim in,
pheromones for the septa

of men and of women.

***

If my daddy isn't gone
and I smell his strength and care
I won't grow my secret hair
till a few years later on
on Tasmania. Down there.

***

When I was pregnant
says your sister, my nose
suddenly went acute:
I smelled which jars and cartons
were opened, rooms away,
which neighbours were in oestrus,
the approach of death in sweat.
I smelt termites in house-framing
all through a town, that mealy taint.
It all became as terrible
as completely true gossip
would be. Then it faded,
as if my baby had learned
enough, and stopped its
strange unhuman education.

***

A teaspoon upside down
in your mouth, and chopping onions
will bring no tears to your cheeks.
The spoon need not be silver.

***

Draw the cork from the stoic age
and the nose is beer and whisky.
I'll drink wine and call myself sensitive!
was a jeer. And it could be risky.

Wesleyans boiled wine for Communion;
a necked paper bag was a tramp;
one glass of sweet sherry at Christmas,
one flagon for the fringe-dwellers' camp.

You rise to wine or you sink to it
was always its Anglo bouquet.

***

When we marched against the government
it would use its dispersant gas
Skunk Hour. Wretched, lingering experience.
When we marched on the neo-feudal
top firms, they sprayed an addictive
fine powder of a thousand hip names
that was bliss in your nostrils, in your head.
Just getting more erased our other causes

and it was kept illegal, to be dear,
and you could destroy yourself to buy it
or beg with your hands through the mesh,
self-selecting, as their chemists did say.

***

Mars having come nearest our planet
the spacecraft Beagle Two went
to probe and sniff and scan it
for life’s irrefutable scent,
the gas older than bowels: methane,
strong marker of digestion from the start,
life-soup-thane, amoeba-thane, tree-thane.

Sensors would screen Ares’ bouquet
for paleo- or present micro-fartlets,
even one-in-a-trillion pico-partlets,
so advanced is the state of the art.
As Mars lit his match in high darkness
Beagle Two was jetting his way.

***

In the lanes of Hautgout
where foetor is rank
Gog smites and Pong strikes
black septums of iron
to keep the low down.
Ride through, nuzzle your pomander:

Don't bathe, I am come to Town:

Far ahead, soaps are rising,
bubble baths and midday soaps.
Death to Phew, taps for Hoh!
Cribs from your Cologne water.

***

Ylang ylang
elan élan
the nostril caves
that breathe stars in
and charm to Spring
the air du temps
tune wombs to sync
turn brut men on
Sir Right, so wrong–
scent, women's sense
its hunters gone
not its influence!
nose does not close
adieu sagesse

DEATH FROM EXPOSURE

That winter. We missed her stark face
at work. Days till she was found, under

his verandah. Even student torturers

used to go in awe. She had zero small talk.

It made no sense she had his key.
It made no sense all she could have

done. Depression exhausts the mind.
She phones, no response, she drives up

straight to his place in the mountains,
down a side road, frost all day.

You knock. What next? You can't manage
what next. Back at last, he finds her car.

She's crawled in, under, among the firewood.
Quite often the world is not round.

ME AND JE REVIENS

My great grand-uncle invented haute couture.
Tiens,
I am related to Je Reviens!

It is the line of Worth, Grandmother's family
that excuses me from chic. It's been done for me.

When Worths from Coolongolook, Aboriginal and
white,
came out of Fromelles trenches on leave from the
fight

they went up to Paris and daringly located
the House of Worth. At the doors, they hesitated–

but were swept from inquiry to welcome to
magnificence:
You have come around the world to rescue France,

dear cousins. Nothing is too good for you!
Feast now and every visit. Make us your
rendezvous.

I checked this with Worths, the senior ones still
living:
Didn't you know that? they said. *Don't you know*
anything?

PRESSURE

A man with a neutral face
in the great migration
clutching his shined suitcase
queueing at the Customs station:

Please (yes, you) open your suitcase.
He may not have understood.
Make it snappy. Open it! Come on!
Looking down out of focus did no good.

Tell him to open his suitcase!
The languages behind him were pressure.

He hugged his case in stark reluctance.
Tell him put suitcase on the counter!

Hasps popped, cut cords fell clear
and there was nothing in the suitcase.

CHURCH

i. m. Joseph Brodsky

The wish to be right
has decamped in large numbers
but some come to God
in hopes of being wrong.

High on the end wall hangs
the Gospel, from before he was books.
All judging ends in his fix,
all, including his own.

He rose out of Jewish,
not English evolution
and he said the lamp he held
aloft to all nations was Jewish.

Freedom still eats freedom,
justice eats justice, love–
even love. One retarded man said
church makes me want to be naughty,

but naked in a muddy trench
with many thousands, someone's saying
the true god gives his flesh and blood.
Idols demand yours off you.

PASTORAL SKETCH

The sex of a stallion at rest
bulges in subtle fine rehearsal,
and his progeny drop in the grass
like little loose bagpipes.
Wet nap and knotty drones, they lie
glazing, and learning air
then they lever upright, wobbling.
Narrow as two dimensions
they nuzzle their mothers' groin
for the yoghurt that makes girth.

BIRTHPLACE

Right in that house over there
an atom of sharp spilled my sanctum
and I was extruded, brain cuff,
in my terror, in my soap.

My heart wrung its two
already working hands together
but all the other animals
started waking up in my body,

the stale-water frog, the starving-worm;
my nerves' knotwork globe
was filling up with panic writing;
bat wings in my chest caught fire

and I screamed in comic hiccups
all before focus, in the blazing cold–
then I was re-plugged, amid soothe,
on to a new blood that tasted.

Nothing else intense
happened to us, in this village.
My two years' schooltime here
were my last in my own culture,

the one I still get held to
in this place, in working hours.
I love the wry equal humane
and drive in to be held to it.

PANIC ATTACK

The body had a nightmare.
Awake. No need of the movie.

No need of light, to keep hips
and shoulders rotating in bed
on the gimbals of wet eyes.

Pounding heart, chest pains–

should it be the right arm hurting?

The brain was a void
or a blasted-out chamber–
shreds of speech in there,
shatters of lust and prayer.

No one can face their heart
or turn their back on it.

Bowel stumbled to bowl,
emptied, and emptied again
till the gut was a train
crawling in its own tunnel,

slowly dragging the nightmare
down with it, below heart level.
You would not have died

the fear had been too great
but: to miss the ambulance moment–

Relax. In time, your hourglass
will be reversed again.

RIPE IN THE ARBOURS OF THE NOSE

Even rippled with sun
the greens of a citrus grove darken
like ocean deepening from shore.

Each tree is full of shade.

A shadowy fast spiral through
and a crow's transfixed an orange
to carry off and mine
its latitudes and longitudes
till they're a parched void scrotum.

alAndalus has an orange grove
planted in rows and shaven above
to form an unwalkable dream lawn
viewed from loggias. One level down,
radiance in a fruit-roofed ambulatory.

Mandarin, if I didn't eat you
How could you ever see the sun?
(Even I will never see it
except in blue translation).

Shedding its spiral pith helmet
an orange is an irrigation
of rupture and bouquet
rocking the lower head about;

one of the milder borders
of the just endurable
is the squint taste of a lemon,

and it was limes, of dark tooled green
which forgave the barefoot sailors

bringing citrus to new dry lands.

Cumquat, you bitter quip,
let a rat make jam of you
in her beardy house.

Blood orange, children!
raspberry blood in the glass:
look for the five o'clock shadow
on their cheeks. Those are full of blood,
and easy: only pick the ones that
relax off in your hand.

Below Hollywood, as everywhere
the trees of each grove appear
as fantastically open
treasure sacks, tied only at the ground.

FROM A TOURIST JOURNAL

In a precinct of liver stone, high
on its dais, the Taj seems bloc hail.

We came to Agra over honking roads
being built under us, past baby wheat
and undoomed beasts and walking people.
Lorries shouldered white marble loads.

Glamour of ads demeaned street life
in the city; many buildings were

held aloft with liverwurst mortar.
I have not left the Taj Mahal.

Camels were lozenge-clipped like rug pile
and workhorses had kept their stallionhood
even in town, around the Taj wall.
Anglos deny theirs all Bollywood.

On Indian streets, tourists must still
say too much no, and be diminished.
Pedlars speak of it to their lit thumbs.
I have not left the Taj Mahal.

Poor men, though, in Raj-time uniforms:
I'd felt that lure too, and understood.
In Delhi, we craned up at a sky-high
sandstone broom cinched with balustrades.

Schoolkids from Nagaland posed with us
below it, for their brag books, and new cars
streamed left and right to the new world,
but from Agra Fort we'd viewed, through haze,

perfection as a factory making depth,
pearl chimneys of the Taj Mahal.

THE CONVERSATIONS

A full moon always rises at sunset
and a person is taller at night.

Many fear their phobias more than death.
The glass King of France feared he'd shatter.
Chinese eunuchs kept their testes in spirit.

Your brain can bleed from a sneeze-breath.
A full moon always rises at sunset
and a person is taller when prone.
Donald Duck was once banned in Finland
because he didn't wear trousers,

his loins were feather-girt like Daisy's
but no ostrich hides its head in sand.
The cure for scurvy was found
then long lost through medical theory.
The Beginning is a steady white sound.

The full moon rises at sunset
and lemurs and capuchin monkeys
pass a millipede round to get off on
its powerful secretions. Mouthing it
they wriggle in bliss on the ground.

The heart of a groomed horse slows down.
A fact is a small compact faith,
a sense-datum to beasts, a power to man
even if true, even while true–
we read these laws in Isaac Neurone.

One woman had sixty-nine children.
Some lions mate fifty times a day.

Napoleon had a victory addiction.
A full moon always rises at sunset.
Soldiers now can get in the family way.

AS COUNTRY WAS SLOW

for Peter

Our new motorway
is a cross-country fort
and we reinforcements
speed between earthworks
water-sumps and counterscarps,
breaking out on wide glimpses,
flying the overpasses–

Little paper lanterns
march up and down dirt,
wrapped round three chopsticks
plastic shrub-guards grow bushes
to screen the real bush,
to hide the old towns
behind sound-walls and green–

Wildlife crossings underneath
the superglued pavement
are jeep size; beasts must see
nature restart beyond.
The roads are our nature
shining beyond delay,

fretting to race on–

Any check in high speed
can bleed into gravel
and hang pastel wreaths
over roadside crosses.
Have you had your scare yet?–
It made you a driver
not an ever-young name.

We're one Ireland, plus
at least six Great Britains
welded around Mars
and cross-linked by cars–
Benzene, diesel, autobahn:
they're a German creation,
these private world-splicers.

The uncle who farmed our place
was an Arab of his day
growing fuel for the horses
who hauled the roads then.
1914 ended that. Will I
see fuel crops come again?
I'll ride a slow vehicle

before cars are slow
as country was slow.

MIDI

Muscles and torsoes of cloud
ascended over the mountains.
The fields looked like high speed
so new-mown was the hay,

then the dark blue Italian lavender
met overhead, a strange maize
deeply planted as mass javelins
in the hoed floor of the land.

Insects in plastic armour stared
from their turrets, and munched
as others machined stiffly over us
and we turned, enchanted
in sweet walling breath
under far-up gables of the lavender.

OBSERVING THE MUTE CAT

Clean water in the house
but the cat laps up clay water
outside. Drinking the earth.

His pile, being perfect,
ignores the misting rain.

A charcoal Russian
he opens his mouth like other cats

and mimes a greeting mew.

At one bound top-speed across
the lawn and halfway up
the zippy pear tree. Why? Branches?
Stopping puzzles him.

Eloquent of purr
or indignant tail
he politely hates to be picked up.
His human friend never does it.

He finds a voice
in the flyscreen, rattling it,
hanging cruciform on it,
all to be let in
to walk on his man.

He can fish food pellets
out of the dispenser, but waits,
preferring to be served.

A mouse he was playing
on the grass ran in under him.
Disconsolate, at last he wandered
off – and drew and fired
himself in one motion.

He is often above you
and appears where you will go.

He swallows his scent, and
discreet with his few stained birds
he carries them off to read.

NURSING HOME

Ne tibi supersis:
don't outlive yourself,
panic, or break a hip
or spit purée at the staff
at the end of gender,
never a happy ender–

yet in the pastel light
of indoors, there is a lady
who has distilled to love
beyond the fall of memory.

She sits holding hands
with an ancient woman
who calls her *brother* and *George*
as bees summarise the garden.

FAME

We were at dinner in Soho
and the couple at the next table
rose to go. The woman paused to say
to me: *I just wanted you to know*

I have got all your cook books
and I swear by them!

I managed
to answer her: *Ma'am*
they've done you nothing but good!
which was perhaps immodest
of whoever I am.

CATTLE-HOOF HARDPAN

Trees from modern times don't bear
but the old China pear
still standing in the soil
of 1880 rains fruit.

PHONE CANVASS

Chatting, after the donation part,
the Blind Society's caller
answered my shy questions:

'...and I love it on the street,
all the echo and air pressure,
people in my forehead and
metal stone brick, the buildings
passing in one side of my head...

I can hear you smiling.'

BROWN SUITS

Sorting clothes for movie costume,
chocolate suits of bull-market cut,
slim blade ties ending in fringes,
brimmed felt hats, and the sideburned
pork-pie ones that served them. I lived then.

The right grade of suit coat, unbuttoned
can still get you a begrudged free meal
in a café. But seat sweat off sunned vinyl,
ghostly through many dry-cleans
and the first deodorants. I lived then

and worked for the man who abolished
bastards. The prime minister who
said on air *I'm what you call a bastard.*
Illegitimate. And drove a last stake
through that lousiest distinction.

EUCALYPTS IN EXILE

They've had so many jobs:
boiling African porridge. Being printed on.
Sopping up malaria. Flying in Paris uprisings.
Supporting a stork's nest in Spain.

Their suits are neater abroad,
of denser drape, un-nibbled:
they've left their parasites at home.

They flower out of bullets
and, without any taproot,
draw water from way deep.
Blown down in high winds
they reveal the black sun of that trick.

Standing around among shed limbs
and loose craquelure of bark
is home-country stuff
but fire is ingrained.
They explode the mansions of Malibu
because to be eucalypts
they have to shower sometimes in Hell.

Their humans, meeting them abroad,
often grab and sniff their hands.

Loveable singly or unmarshalled
they are merciless in a gang.

CHERRIES FROM YOUNG

Cherries from Young
that pretty town,
white cherries and black,
sun-windows on them.

Cherries from Young
the tastiest ever
grow in drought time

on farms above there.

One lip-teased drupe
or whole sweet gallop
poured out of cardboard
in whatever year,

cherries from Young.
All the roads back
go down into Young
that early town.

HIGH-SPEED BIRD

At full tilt, air gleamed–
and a window-struck kingfisher,
snatched up, lay on my palm
still beating faintly.

Slowly, a tincture
of whatever consciousness is
infused its tremor, and
ram beak wide as scissors

all hurt loganberry inside,
it crept over my knuckle
and took my outstretched finger
in its wire foot-rings.

Cobalt wings, shutting on beige

body. Gold under-eye whiskers,
beak closing in recovery
it faced outward from me.

For maybe twenty minutes
we sat together, one on one,
as if staring back or
forward into prehistory.

THE FARM TERRACES

Beautiful merciless work
around the slopes of earth
terraces cut by curt hoe
at the orders of hunger
or a pointing lord.
Levels eyed up to rhyme
copied from grazing animals
round the steeps of earth,
balconies filtering water
down stage to stage of drop.
Wind-stirred colours of crop
swell between walked bunds
miles of grass-rimmed contour
harvests down from the top
by hands long in the earth.
Baskets of rich made soil
boosted up poor by the poor,
ladder by freestone prop
stanzas of chant-long lines

by backwrenching slog, before
money, gave food and drunk
but rip now like slatted sails
(some always did damn do)
down the abrupts of earth.

RUGBY WHEELS

i.m. Matt Laffan 1970–2009

Four villages in Ireland
knew never to mix their blood
but such lore gets lost
in the emigrations.
Matt Laffan's parents learned it
in their marriage of genes

they could never share again.
They raised Matt through captaincies
and law degrees. And he exalted them
with his verve and clarities,
sat on a rugby tribunal,
drank beers a third his height

and rode a powered wheelchair
akimbo as in a chariot
with tie-clip, combed red hair,
causes to plead. Beloved in Sydney
he created a travel website
for the lame, and grinned among them

Doors will often open.
Beware a step or two
down or up when they do,
and he told self-doubters
You'll always be taller than me!
as he flew his electoral box-kite.

Popular with women, and yet
vision of him in their company
often shows a precipice near
or a balcony-lit corridor.
I would have lacked his
heroism in being a hero.

HESIOD ON BUSHFIRE

Poxes of the Sun or of the mind
bring the force-ten firestorms.
After come same-surname funerals,
junked theory, praise of mateship.

Love the gum forest, camp out in it
but death hosts your living in it, brother.
You need buried space
and cellars have a convict foetor:

only pubs kept them. Houses shook them off
wherever Diggers moved to.
Only opal desert digs homes by dozer,
the cool Hobbit answer.

Cellars, or bunkers, mustn't sit square
under the fuel your blazing house will be,
but nearby, roofed refractory,
tight against igniting air-miles.

Power should come underground
from Fortress Suburbia, and your treasures
stay back there, where few now
grow up in the fear of grass.

Never build on a summit or a gully top:
fire's an uphill racer deliriously welcomed
by growth it cures of growth.
Shun a ridgeline, window puncher at a thousand
 degrees.

Sex is Fire, in the ancient Law.
Investment is Fire. Grazing beasts are cool Fire
backburning paddocks to the door.
Ideology is Fire.

The British Isles and giant fig trees are Water.
Horse-penis helicopters are watery TV
but unblocked roads and straight volunteers
are lifesaving spume spray.

Water and Fire chase each other in jet
planes. May you never flee through them
at a generation's end, as when
the Great Depression died, or Marvellous Melbourne.

PORT JACKSON GREASEPROOF ROSE

Which spawned more civilisations,
yellow grass or green?

Who made poverty legal?
Who made poverty at all?

Eating a cold pork sandwich
out of greaseproof paper
as I cross to Circular Quay
where the world-ships landed poverty
on the last human continent
where it had not been known.

Linked men straddling their chains
being laughed at by naked people.

This belongs to my midlife:
out of my then suburban city
rise towers of two main kinds,
new glass ones keyed high to catch money
and brown steeples to forgive the poor

who made poverty illegal
and were sentenced here for it.
The naked here were shot for it.

And the first jumbo jets descend
like mates whose names you won't recall,

going down behind the city.

THE BLAME

for Clare

Archie was a gun to shoot at biplanes
and an uncle I missed meeting, a dancing whiz
till we lost the footwork that was his.

His elder brother was a timbercutter
who scorned to fell a rotting tree
so their father wheedled hapless Archie

who dropped it crooked, into his brain.
All would rather he had left children
on earth than the mighty grief that followed.

His mother had seen the head-splash happen
five hours before it did, and rode
searching the bush to find the men.

She saw because she knew her world.
Later she would ask her husband
Did you even take your own axe, Allan?

Face and bequests were the family-labour system
so the expert brother got his owed block
with a weatherproof dairy and bung clock.

Everything else let the wind through.
Neither he nor his father believed in accident.
Punishment was happening. He was charged rent

to preclude any loans for farm improvement.
Some had always scorned his town wife's dignity
and his brother's name cried out in dreams.

He, the blamed son, loved all his mother gave him,
the gold watch, touring car, touch of fey;
the latter two failed on his wife's death day

but the car was kept till it fell apart.
Archie's name was shunned, its luck was bad,
but all his survivors got the farm we'd had.

Now nearly everyone who knew an Archie
has gone to join him in memory.
Freed of blood, the name starts to return.

THE MIRRORBALL

Half a day's drive from Melbourne
until we reach the first town
that's not bypassed by expressway.
Holbrook, once Germantown,
Holbrook of the submarines,
conning tower and periscopes
rising out of sheep land.

It recalls the country towns
up the roads of 1940
each with its trees and Soldier,
its live and dead shop windows
and a story like Les Boyce
we heard about up home,
Taree's Lord Mayor of London.

But now song and story are pixels
of a mirrorball that spins celebrities
in patter and tiny music
so when the bus driver restarts
his vast tremolo of glances
half his earplugged sitters wear
the look of deserted towns.

INFINITE ANTHOLOGY

Gross motor – co-ordination as a whistle subject
audiation – daydreaming in tunes
papped – snapped by paparazzi
whipping side – right hand side of a convict or sheep
hepcat, hip (from Wolof *hipi-kat,* one who knows the
score)– spirit in which modernist art goes slumming
instant – (Australian) Nescafé
ranga – redhead

Creators of single words or phrases are by far the largest class of poets. Many ignore all other poetry.

Jail tats – totemic underskin writing done because illegal
lundy – a turned Ulster
rebuttal tapes – counter-propaganda filmed by warplanes
free traders – (19th and early 20th cent.) split bloomers worn under voluminous skirts
daylight – second placegetter when winner is very superior to field
window licker – a voyeur
fibro – resident of a poorer suburb

Single-word poets hope to be published and credited in the Great Book of Anon, the dictionary. The cleverest make their names serve this purpose: Maxim, Maxim's, Churchillian.

Irishtown – a Soweto of old-time Catholic labour
bunny boiler – one who kills her offspring
dandruff acting – the stiffest kind of Thespian art
blackout – Aboriginal party or picnic, whites not invited
butternut – homespun cloth dyed with hickory juice
shart – a non-dry fart
Baptist Boilermaker – coffee and soda (an imagined Puritan cocktail)

Single-word poets recycle words in advance of need, or leave them exposed to the weather of real difference.

Wedge – cloth bunched in the groin; may cause camel toe
(q.v.)
wedge – to force the pace or direction
bushed – lost (Australian)
bushed – tired (American)
bushed – suffering camp fever (Canadian)
limo – limousin cattle
proud – castrated but still interested

Many quaint items are invented merely for show, but similar items may be the insignia of particular groups or classes.

Drummy – echoing, hollow-sounding (mining term)
rosebud – American Civil War wound
Shabos goy – Gentile who does small jobs for Orthodox Jews on Sabbath or other holy days
choke – to strap loose freight tightly together for transport
off book – (theatre) having one's lines down pat
bugle driver – attachment on a drill to intensify its power in sinking screws
tipping elbow – (Aboriginal) sneaking glances at one's watch

MANUSCRIPT ROUNDEL

What did you see in the walnut?
Horses red-harnessed criss cross

and a soldier wearing the credits
of his movie like medal ribbons.
An egg in there building a buttery
held itself aloft in its hands–
red straps then pulled the nut shut.

NATAL GRASS

Plain as wicker most of the year
along October this tousled grass
wakes up on road verges in a smoke
of sago bloom, of ginger knots
tied in a shapeless woolly plasma

but get this web across the sun
and it ignites cut-glass rosé
goblets and pitchers. In God's name
liquid opal from a parallel shore,
the dazzle of dew anytime of day.

Front Cover Flap

From his life's work so far, spanning more than four decades, Les Murray has selected these 100 poems, his personal best. Including classics such as 'The Broad Bean Sermon', 'An Absolutely Ordinary Rainbow' and 'The Dream of Wearing Shorts Forever', this collection is guaranteed to delight Murray fans and introduce new readers to his work. It is a treasure trove of the best poems ever written in Australia.

'There is no poetry in the English language now so rooted in its sacredness, so broadleafed in its pleasures and yet so intimate and conversational.'

DEREK WALCOTT

Back Cover Flap

Les Murray is Australia's leading poet. He lives in Bunyah, near Taree in New South Wales. He has published some thirty books. His work is studied in schools and universities around Australia and has been translated into many foreign languages. In 1996 he was awarded the T.S. Eliot Prize for poetry, in 1999 the Queen's Gold Medal for poetry, and in 2004 the Mondello Prize.

Back Cover Material

'No poet has ever travelled like this, whether in reality or simply in mind ... Seeing the shape or hearing the sound of one thing in another, he finds forms'

CLIVE JAMES

Made in the USA
Lexington, KY
11 June 2019